IN
OUR
FIFTIES

IN OUR FIFTIES

VOICES OF MEN AND WOMEN REINVENTING THEIR LIVES

WILLIAM H. BERGQUIST
ELINOR MILLER GREENBERG
G. ALAN KLAUM

Jossey-Bass Publishers
San Francisco

Substantial discounts on bulk quantities of Jossey-Bass books
are available to corporations, professional associations, and other
organizations. For details and discount information, contact the
special sales department at Jossey-Bass Inc., Publishers.
(415) 433-1740; Fax (415) 433-0499.

For sales outside the United States, contact Maxwell Macmillan
International Publishing Group, 866 Third Avenue, New York,
New York 10022.

Manufactured in the United States of America

The paper used in this book is acid-free and meets the
State of California requirements for recycled paper
(50 percent recycled waste, including 10 percent
postconsumer waste), which are the strictest guidelines
for recycled paper currently in use in the United States.

10% POST
CONSUMER
WASTE

The ink in this book is either soy- or vegetable-based and during the
printing process emits fewer than half the volatile organic compounds
(VOCs) emitted by petroleum-based ink.

Library of Congress Cataloging-in-Publication Data

Bergquist, William H.
   In our fifties : voices of men and women reinventing their lives /
William H. Bergquist, Elinor Miller Greenberg, G. Alan Klaum. — 1st
ed.
     p.   cm.
   Includes bibliographical references and index.
   ISBN 1-55542-513-5
   1. Middle aged persons—United States. 2. Middle aged persons—
United States—Psychology. I. Greenberg, Elinor. II. Klaum, G.
Alan, date. III. Title.
HQ1059.5.U5B37 1993
305.24'4—dc20   92-46044
                                            CIP

FIRST EDITION
HB Printing   10 9 8 7 6 5 4 3 2 1   *Code 9327*

*To those courageous men and
women in their fifties who continue
to reinvent themselves, giving their
lives—and ours—new and richer
meaning.*

CONTENTS

Preface   xi

The Authors   xix

1. Myths and Realities: The Invisible Decade   1

2. New Identities, New Priorities: Settling Down or Gearing Up?   11

3. Stories and Dreams: Listening to Inner Voices   27

4. Body and Mind: Over the Hill or In Our Prime?   40

5. The Mirror of History: Understanding Commonality and Diversity   55

6. Friends and Lovers: The Quest for Relationship and Autonomy   75

7. Families: New Roles as Parents, Grandparents, and Children   89

8. Work and Career: Changing Needs and
   Sources of Meaning   115

9. Leadership: Power, Redefinition, and
   Self-Renewal   136

10. Achievement and Failure: Coming to Terms   148

11. Reinventing Our Lives: The Challenge of
    Change   165

12. To the Next Generation: Preparing for Your
    Fifties   173

    Appendix: Research Questions   183

    Recommended Readings   185

    Notes   189

    Index   195

PREFACE

There are many nagging questions about being between the ages of fifty and sixty in our rapidly changing society. Perhaps such questions are too sensitive or too threatening to be explored openly, but they are familiar questions to most men and women now in their fifties who are thinking about what lies ahead:

- Is it too late to start over?
- What can I do to take charge of my own life?
- Will I face a major illness?
- Will I keep my job or will I be forced to retire?
- Will I have enough money?
- Will I need to compromise on my goals and ambitions?
- Who will want me, need me, or love me when I'm over fifty?
- How does the life I am now living compare to the lives of other men and women my age?

Many of these questions frighten us because they reach down to the very core of our identities. Yet the decade in our lives in which we try to answer these questions and assert our identities has been largely invisible, undiscussed, and unexplored.

As increasing numbers of us live longer, healthier lives and as the massive group of baby boomers begins to approach their fifties, many of us feel an urgent need not only to explore and understand our midlife years but also to regenerate and reinvent our lives. *In Our Fifties* turns a spotlight on this invisible decade. We three authors, who are also in our fifties, have interviewed many men and women between fifty and sixty. We have examined our own experiences and discussed this "hidden" decade with many others in order to discover what we in our fifties have in common and where and how we are likely to differ from each other. Among these varied experiences we have found strategies to make this decade rich and rewarding.

Audience

This book is written for men and women who are approaching the end of their fifties and want to understand what has happened to them during this era, those in the middle of this decade who are still exploring their fifties journey, and those who are just beginning their fifties and want to make the most of these potentially productive years.

We also write to the large group of Americans nicknamed the "baby boomers" — the men and women who will be entering their fifties prior to the turn of the century. This group, now in or approaching their forties, will soon provide the primary leadership for our society. We hope the insights recently acquired by their slightly older sisters and brothers will assist them to prepare for their important leadership tasks.

We also hope that this book will encourage researchers, teachers, and students to pursue a more extensive scientific exploration of this profound and fascinating decade in which many people come to make crucial personal choices that shape the rest of their lives.

Learning About Our Fifties

Traditionally, most of us in this society have looked to our elders to provide us with wisdom and guidance. But in our rapidly changing world, is it realistic to expect our parents or other people who have already lived through their fifties to be our models? Certainly, the stories our parents have to tell us about their lives during their fifties can be sources of some insight, and we can also reflect back on our direct observations of our parents' actions and emotions during this period of their lives.

Still, the experiences of our elders seem different from our own experience of our fifties. The memories and models of our parents' generation no longer seem sufficient to guide us through the sometimes confusing changes occurring in our own families, our work, and our sense of self. Our society's dramatic shifts in values, advances in medicine, transformations in jobs, changes in childrearing patterns, and ideas of what makes a family mean that we encounter a different set of problems and potentials in our fifties today.

As we searched for sources to learn about our fifties decade, it became clear to us as authors that we needed to explore beyond our own personal and professional experiences and talk to other men and women in their fifties. Only through sharing many experiences could we identify the major themes of our fifties decade, create a structure for integrating these themes, and communicate key messages and lessons for people to use.

Our Study

In the years from 1987 to 1991, we conducted a study of seventy-three men and women between the ages of fifty and sixty. Each of these men and women was interviewed for one to three hours and was asked to reflect and comment on a variety of life issues ranging from friendship to careers and from sexuality to spirituality. (The interview questions are listed in the Appendix.) The interviewers were advanced doctoral students attending the Professional School of Psychology in San Francisco and in Sacramento, California. Because the school specializes in educating mature adults, the average interviewer was both considerably older (ages thirty-five and over) and more experienced than the typical graduate student.

Our study was not intended to be a statistical one; however, we did seek relative diversity in the interview group. Sixty-five of the interviews were with people of European-American origin. In addition, four Hispanics, two African Americans, one Japanese American, and one Asian Indian were interviewed. Most of the interviewees had middle-class backgrounds, although six were from the lower socioeconomic levels of our society. We assume that most of the men and women we interviewed were heterosexual; only three people (two men and one woman) identified themselves as homosexual.

The careers of the women interviewed were highly varied. Thirteen of the forty-three women identified themselves as housewives who did not work outside the home. Four women were teachers; five worked in corporations as managers, secretaries, or clerks; five were employed in social or health service organizations and two in the government; one worked in a small nonprofit organization; and nine were entrepreneurs or self-employed professionals. The occupations of the remaining four women were not clearly defined.

Of the thirty men we studied, seven worked in corporate or other business settings, usually in management or sales. Four were teachers and four were in social or health service positions. The others were a tree maintenance expert, an engineer, a jazz musician, a painter, a priest, a retired military officer, an actor, a state worker, and a variety of entrepreneurs.

Many previous studies of adult development have focused on only one gender, usually males. In this study, we hope to establish an important precedent by building a model of middle-class adult life in the years from fifty to sixty that includes the voices of both men and women. Our study also reflects the increasing proportion of women in our society as our population, as a whole, ages.

Eleven percent of the people we interviewed were from minority ethnic populations, and, with the exception of one person from New York City, all the people we interviewed lived in California. However, this regional bias is mitigated by the fact that many of the interviews were conducted in the Sacramento area — a region representative of the U.S. mainstream with regard to people's values, aspirations, economic status, and life-styles. In addition, many of those interviewed had previously lived in other parts of the United States. Although the impact of this fact was not explored in the study, we believe it reduces the regional bias of our findings.

The ultimate test of our exploratory search for the ways in which fifty- to sixty-year-old men and women in the United States think, feel, and behave will come as our readers look for themselves in these pages. We offer observations rather than norms and prescriptions, but we believe we have painted a representative portrait of middle-class midlife men and women. We also believe that our findings show the remarkable challenges and opportunities of being fifty in the world of today.

Overview of the Contents

In Chapter One, we will explore the invisibility of the fifties decade, the differing perspectives of men and women, and the various views about what is most important at this stage of life. We also discover why we need new myths to give us form and meaning and why we must think in terms of reinventing ourselves.

In Chapters Two through Five, we will see the ways in which the people who were interviewed struggle with and find fulfillment within themselves during their fifties. The focus is on the self, on examining our images of ourselves, our changing priorities, our emerging inner life, and our potential for a new vitality. We will pay particular attention to the similarities and differences between the ways men and women see themselves. We also look at the popular culture that shaped our childhood and adolescent expectations and at the massive cultural shifts that both tested and reshaped those expectations.

In Chapters Six and Seven, we turn from our images of ourselves to our relationships with others. We will view men's and women's searches for both community and autonomy and

for new ways of relating to our spouses and lovers, our grown
children and aging parents, and our children's children.

Next, in Chapters Eight through Ten, we focus on the ways
in which men and women find, or fail to find, fulfillment in the
external community. How do we find meaning in our work and
careers? How do we assert authority and leadership? How do
we come to terms with lifetime achievements and failures?

Last of all, we look to the future, our future. Chapter
Eleven challenges our peers in this age group to explore themselves deeply in order to search for a more authentic self. Readers
are urged to reevaluate and reinvent their lives, using the wise
and mature insights of their recent years, and to engage in new
forms of leadership and civic responsibility.

Chapter Twelve is addressed to the men and women who
will soon be following all of us through the fifties decade — the
"baby boomers," born between 1946 and 1964. Now in or approaching their forties, they grew up "in the best of times," which
turned to times of personal disillusionment and national conflict.
The authors' open letter to the baby boomers presents our four
key messages about choices, supports, generative activities, and
integrity that apply to all people in their fifties.

The Appendix presents the questions that the interviewers
asked of the seventy-three participants in our study. The Recom-
mended Readings section provides a list of books that we have
found to be relevant to the fifties years and that readers may
likewise find of interest. Finally, the Notes section points readers
to the information sources we used in writing the book.

We did not approach this book with preconceived theories about what we would find. We came to our conclusions
by exploring the ideas of recognized scholars and writers who
preceded us in this field, by examining the concerns, themes,
and messages generated by our interviews with others in their
fifties, and by discussing all these ideas among ourselves and
with our peers. Therefore, *In Our Fifties* is itself a mirror of the
processes and dialogues we recommend to other men and women
as they explore their own fifties. The processes include study,
reflection, sharing, and inquiry. For those of us who have gone
through these processes, the result has been a renewed sense

of coherence, a deeper way of finding meaning in our lives, and the emergence of a powerful personal integrity.

Acknowledgments

This book was born from the efforts of many generous men and women. To those journeying through their fifties who shared their illuminating and moving stories with us — at times through tears, at times with laughter and happiness — our heartfelt thanks. To the community of graduate students from the Professional School of Psychology who participated in the interview process that formed the core of this book and who provided their own unique insights, your work was both professional and commendable. We owe you a special debt of gratitude. It was through you that we learned what the "invisible decade" of the fifties is all about.

We are indebted to many gifted thinkers, scholars, researchers, and clinicians whose own work in the field of adult development has provided us with a remarkable framework from which to see and to explore. Among these are Mary Belenky, Robert Bellah, Warren Bennis, Robert Bly, Arthur Chickering, Erik Erikson, Carol Gilligan, Roger Gould, Carl Jung, Morris T. Keeton, Daniel Levinson, the late Jack Lindquist, William G. Perry, Jr., Gary Quehl, Lillian Ruben, Gail Sheehy, Jill Tarule, their colleagues, and a host of still others.

To our families, friends, and loved ones who watched this book sprout and flower, who provided the support, inspiration, and encouragement across the months, a special note of acknowledgment and gratitude.

Our thanks also to Judy Reed, who managed to coordinate three peripatetic, busy authors in different corners of the planet, for typing the manuscript and for sharing her own journey through her fifties, which provided still more insight and balance. Without her loyal assistance and incomparable computer skills, this book would never have been completed. To three special people — Cliff Cardillo in New York, Barbara Larratt in Connecticut, and Laling Lim in the Philippines — for reading the manuscript as it evolved, whose questions, suggestions, and criticisms prodded us toward greater clarity. To Eunice Kelly and Alan Schut from the Professional School of Psychology for providing their expertise, special humor, and support to our endeavor. To a gifted copyeditor, Elspeth MacHattie, who helped so sensitively reweave our study into its final form. And to a remarkable editor and friend, Becky McGovern, who led us through the process with her colleagues and "brought us home." For these many gifts, we are indeed most grateful.

February 1993   WILLIAM H. BERGQUIST
                                         San Francisco, California

                                         ELINOR MILLER GREENBERG
                                         Littleton, Colorado

                                         G. ALAN KLAUM
                                         San Francisco, California

THE AUTHORS

WILLIAM H. BERGQUIST is president of the Professional School of Psychology in San Francisco and in Sacramento, California. The school specializes in preparing mature men and women for careers in psychology. He received his B.A. degree (1962) from Occidental College and his M.A. (1963) and Ph.D. (1969) degrees from the University of Oregon, all in psychology.

Bergquist has consulted with more than four hundred organizations over the past twenty-five years and has conducted more than one hundred workshops and seminars on life and career planning, life transitions, and personal growth. His most recent books include *The Four Cultures of the Academy* (1992), *Developing Human and Organizational Resources* (1993), and *The Postmodern Organization* (1993). His current research interests include the process of psychological adaptation to strokes and the role of partnerships and sanctuaries in postmodern society.

As a man in his fifties, Bergquist lives with his wife, Kathleen, in a small Northern California coastal community. He is also a proud father and grandfather.

ELINOR MILLER GREENBERG is president and CEO of EMG Associates, a Colorado-based national consulting and publishing firm whose clients include foundations, businesses, government agencies, community organizations, and institutions of higher education. She received her B.A. degree (1953) from Mount Holyoke College in speech and psychology, her M.A. degree (1954) from the University of Wisconsin, Madison, in speech pathology, and her Ed.D. degree (1981) from the University of Northern Colorado, Greeley, in lifelong education. She holds honorary degrees from Saint-Mary-of-the-Woods College in Indiana and the Professional School of Psychology in California.

Greenberg's forty-year career spans work in human relations, community development, college teaching and administration, leadership and organizational development, and women's issues. Her recent research includes studies of undergraduate minority adult students, working adult learners, and women's leadership. Greenberg's books include *Designing Undergraduate Education* (1981, with W. H. Bergquist and R. A. Gould), *New Partnerships: Higher Education and the Nonprofit Sector* (1982, editor and contributor), and *Weaving: The Fabric of a Woman's Life* (1991). She is also a frequent public speaker, radio and television interviewee, and newspaper columnist.

Greenberg has been appointed by Colorado governors Richard D. Lamm and Roy Romer to numerous state government boards and commissions, including the Colorado State Board for Community Colleges and Occupational Education (1981 to 1986) and the Colorado Women's Economic Development Council (1987 to the present), of which she was a founding member. She has been recognized for her contributions to education, human rights, and community development and has received many awards and honors.

Greenberg lives in Littleton, Colorado, with her husband, Manny, of thirty-seven years. Their three grown children live in Colorado, Tennessee, and Texas.

G. ALAN KLAUM is president of Alan Klaum International, a consulting firm that serves corporations and institutions in the areas of systems change, conflict and crisis management, financial and strategic planning, marketing and public relations development, and organizational psychology. He received his B.A. degree (1954) from Columbia University in international affairs, his M.A. degree (1957) from the Fletcher School of Law and Diplomacy, Tufts and Harvard Universities, in international affairs, and his second M.A. degree (1992) from the Professional School of Psychology in organizational and clinical psychology. He is a doctoral candidate at the Professional School of Psychology and is completing his dissertation on a crosscultural study of men and women in their fifties.

Much of Klaum's earlier corporate life in banking, finance, and investment was spent in Asia, the Middle East, and Europe. A journalist, poet, and teacher, he currently serves on the board of directors of the Harlem Spiritual Ensemble in New York and the Institute for Social Research and Psychology, and is co-director of the Sutter Institute in San Francisco. He is deeply committed to education and community development to combat the AIDS epidemic and has worked with the University of California Task Force on AIDS and the Stop AIDS project in Sacramento, California. In addition to his nonprofit corporate consulting, Klaum maintains a private clinical practice.

IN
OUR
FIFTIES

1

Myths and Realities:
The Invisible Decade

All things must change
to something new, to something strange.
— *Henry Wadsworth Longfellow*

If you ask people who are not yet fifty what they think are the primary concerns of those of us in our fifties, you are generally likely to hear a negative view of this decade. They will tell you about retirement, declining health, diminished energy, and coming to terms with the limitations that are imposed by being closer to the end of life than to its beginning.

Yet most contemporary people in the fifties age group are discovering they have a surprisingly positive view of this decade. Their retirement is still a long way off — at least ten or fifteen years. They are often in excellent health and feel youthful and vigorous. Rather than brooding on the limitations of life, today's middle-class fifty-year-olds are likely to be faced with many choices — indeed, they may feel bewildered not by the lack of opportunities but by the abundance.

Why does this come as a surprise? Why have most of us been so far off target in our predictions about our fifties? The answer is quite simple: our fifties are unexplored territory. We have become accustomed to assigning men and women in their forties to that "mid life" period in which they would reach the prime of their careers and prepare for their children's maturation. We think of those in their sixties and seventies as "senior

1

citizens." The large and immensely powerful American Association of Retired Persons (AARP) is open to individuals as soon as they reach their fiftieth birthday, yet its focus is on retirement, Medicare, and other senior citizen issues. We have had no neat descriptive labels, nor even public myths, to describe our fifties. As a transition period between what has been and what is yet to come, this decade has been "invisible." Those who do try to describe it do not agree about it. Less optimistic people may see the glass as half empty and may want to call the fifties the do-or-die decade or last-chance decade. More optimistic individuals may want to call it the generative decade or the decade of maturity. Still others may want to see it as the decade of leadership.

As explorers in this uncharted and disputed territory, we the authors of this book believe this decade is obscure because our society has changed so dramatically during the past twenty years. A half-century ago, fifty-year-old men and women were already retiring and often preparing to die. Today, men and women do not confront these inevitabilities until their sixties, seventies, or even eighties. Because of changes in life-styles, career patterns, and medicine, the decade of our fifties no longer fits into the "old age" category. On the other hand, it is certainly not just a simple extension of middle age. Most of us who are fifty sense this, yet we see little acknowledgment of it anywhere.

Media Myths About Our Fifties

There are very few acknowledged fifty-year-old heroes or heroines on television, in movies, or in novels. While we are inundated with rich and diverse images of twenty-, thirty-, and forty-year-old movie and rock stars—from Julia Roberts to Meryl Streep and from Michael J. Fox to Kevin Costner—we have few images of fifty-year-old stars. Hollywood's older leading men, such as Warren Beatty, Paul Newman, and Robert Redford, seem ageless and are only rarely acknowledged as the fifty- or sixty-year-olds they truly are.

The real ages of such glamourous women as Raquel Welch, Joan Collins, and Elizabeth Taylor are just now beginning to be recognized. Even though the media message about these women is often ambivalent — admiring youthfulness while simultaneously disapproving of their efforts to retain their youthful faces and bodies — it may be that glamour, vitality, and sexuality are beginning to become an acceptable part of the new fifties image. By the time our pace-setting baby boomers reach their fifties, the positive traits of this decade may, indeed, become truly fashionable.

Currently, however, most fifty- to sixty-year-old celebrity women continue to portray stereotypical mothers or eccentric aunts, just as they were once assigned stereotypical roles that emphasized their glamour. Older men, too, are cast primarily as "has beens" or as foolish fathers and grandfathers, reinforcing negative images about our fifties.

The image that lingers, despite the growing number of vital and attractive movie and television stars in their fifties, is that men and women at that age are preparing for a life of physical decline and diminished social recognition and leadership. Themes of sacrifice and stability among fifty- to sixty-year-old people abound because it has been generally viewed as immature for men and women of this age group to actively pursue individual dreams, especially if those dreams have an impact on their economic welfare, their family's future, their choice of friends, or their roles in their communities. It is thought that fifty-year-olds should be shutting down options, not opening them up.

Yet, it is precisely expansion and change that are most prevalent today in the lives of many of the fifty-year-olds that the authors know as friends and colleagues or that we have interviewed. In fact, without this expansion and change, men and women in their fifties become stagnant and ill-prepared for the later decades of their lives.

Therefore, it is time for the old myths to be transformed and for new images to be projected so that we can understand the issues of personal growth that pervade our now dynamic fifties.

The Perspective of Gender

Some important studies on women's development[1] suggest that men and women view each stage of adult life in quite different ways. As we identify new images for our fifties, we need to be aware that both male and female perspectives may come to light.

Some writers have suggested that men tend to become more nurturing in this decade of life while women become more independent and career-oriented. In other words, men and women tend to take on each other's former characteristics. Men, as they grow older, increasingly search for community and connection with other people while women search for increased autonomy. Both men and women, however, feel a need to develop a better understanding of this period in their lives.

Our Need for New Images

During our interviews and conversations, we found that fifty-year-old women (and baby-boomer women) are eager to find books that can serve as a foundation for discussions of their shared experiences of love, work, and self in a changing society. They want to know how other women have raised children or balanced work and childrearing. The prevalent message of some feminist writers, whether intended or not, has been that women should be working outside the home. Women who chose not to do so, for whatever reason, have often come to feel guilty or inadequate, and they want to address these feelings. Women also want to talk about marriage, divorce, separation, and their evolving relationships with men. They are eager to share their anxieties about aging, being left alone, caretaking, and death.

However, they do not look to their mothers for guidance as they would have just a couple of generations ago. Times have changed, and they feel that their mothers' experiences are relatively irrelevant as guides for their own lives. Therefore, they must seek guidance elsewhere in order to avoid the agonies other women in their fifties have experienced while struggling with changing physical and economic conditions, societal expectations, and family relationships. They want a more positive, integrated self-image.

The men we interviewed were also increasingly looking for forums in which they could discuss personal feelings and experiences regarding their fifties, although such forums — whether personally or professionally organized — are still rare in our society. The current generation of fifty-year-old men was not brought up to share personal feelings with others. Nevertheless, men are beginning to shape new images which they can use to better understand their own distinctive life changes.[2]

In a society that expects action and accomplishment from its males, fifty-year-old men often fear a loss of energy and status, of a meaningful social role and recognition. Many men, however, seem to have developed a strong internal drive to overcome their old self-images in order to reduce such fears and to engage their fifties as an exciting era of regeneration and renewal.

More Diversities

Our gender is not the only factor that affects our images and the way we redefine who we are as we grow older. Socioeconomic status, ethnicity, religion, sexual orientation, and cultural origin all play major roles throughout our adult lives and can be particularly important during decades of significant change such as our fifties.

For example, we have chosen to focus on the middle-class mainstream, but among the lower socioeconomic classes in the United States are whole communities of men and women who are preparing for death, not for new life, as they confront their fifties. One of the populations that we had hoped to study for this book was fifty- to sixty-year-old coal miners in West Virginia and Western Pennsylvania. However, we discovered that virtually all the men in this group either were already dead of black lung disease or related ailments, or were in such poor health that they could not be interviewed. Although their wives were often still alive, these women were unwilling to talk much about their lives, for they saw little left to live for or to talk about. We had also hoped to look at the men and women in our society who grew up in comfortable, affluent surroundings and then lost their jobs and security and by their fifties found themselves relegated to the ranks of the homeless. We are curious about the impact such misfortune or misdeeds have upon these individuals as they think of their future.

In his noted study of adult development among men in their forties, Daniel Levinson[3] writes about the lives of men from different walks of life. By the time many of those from the working class have reached their forties, they are developmentally frozen — or worse, they are unemployed, substance abusers, or transients. If their lives and careers have centered on their physical attributes — on manual labor or on athletics and sexual prowess — they are past their peak of popularity and earning power.

Similarly, for women from the working class, the decade of their fifties is often filled with prospects of declining health and lost job opportunities because of their increasing inability to perform manual labor at a satisfactory level. They have lost status as breadwinners and often as mothers and lovers. Even recreation for these women is often lacking or distorted. As Lillian Rubin notes, these people turn everywhere and often find only a "world of pain."[4]

Of course, life for some men and women from the working class is, at times, filled with great personal satisfaction. But too often, they are not only living in an invisible decade, they are also members of a class that is often invisible in our society. However, even though the themes and messages in this book are drawn from middle-class men and women, many of them apply to low-income men and women as well. As new images for our fifties are accepted and as social attitudes toward fifty-year-olds become more positive, working-class men and women will also benefit. Their challenge will be greater than that faced by others of the middle class, but once some individuals blaze the trail, the goal of continuing to grow and change will become one we can all share, even if we achieve it by different paths.

Reinventing Ourselves

At the heart of the matter for those of us in our fifties, no matter what our backgrounds, is the need to consider reinventing ourselves. Each of us goes about this task in his or her own unique and appropriate way, yet we can also view it in general terms.

Erik Erikson, one of the leading figures in psychoanalysis and human development, sees our fifties as the beginning of a life-cycle phase that he terms *matured adulthood.* During this period, men and women have to start dealing with a growing tension between generativity and stagnation. By *generativity* Erikson means taking care of all that has been procreated, produced, and created. It is "a vital strength of care," a "widening concern for what has been generated by love, necessity, or accident; it overcomes the ambivalence arising from irreversible obligation. Thus, [it] attends to the needs of all that has been generated."[5] Generativity is growth-producing development, a strong desire both to teach and to learn about those many aspects of life that offer excitement and challenge. *Stagnation,* on the other hand, is acceptance of the status quo and a refusal to grow. While all of us must sustain some aspects of our old selves as we reinvent our new selves, the decade of our fifties is no time for merely continuing the old, for to do so invariably leads to this personal stagnation. Instead, we must master the difficult balancing act between our old selves and our new, emerging selves in order to continue our adult development.

In our fifties, work and career often become our foundation for either generativity or stagnation. In making decisions about their work in their fifties, wise men and women will seek work environments and career paths that present new challenges and new learning opportunities. The road to generativity is paved, in part, by work that has intrinsic meaning, no matter where it is performed — at home; in an office, store, or production plant; or on the road. It is not how our work is seen by others that is important; it is the meaning of our own work to ourselves that is the measure of its potential for generativity.

Because reinvention involves a struggle to assess and come to grips with the caring portion of self, it leads many to move beyond immediate personal concerns and to assume new responsibilities for the welfare of future generations and the community at large. However, Erikson warns us that inherent in this shift of concern are two basic dangers: a "maladaptive" and a "malignant" tendency. The maladaptive tendency occurs when we extend caring beyond our individual capacity to handle it.

The malignant tendency occurs when we end up simply not caring to care for anybody.[6] To remain vital to the end of our life journey is a noble task, but one fraught with difficult choices and potential dangers.

Some of the people interviewed for this book had left everything behind in the process of reinvention. They had dissociated themselves from everything that existed in their past and were trying to become a new kind of person leading an entirely new kind of life. We have mixed feelings about turning one's back completely on one's old life and wonder how these people will fare in the future. We believe that there are ways to retain the valuable aspects of our prior selves and that men and women in their fifties do not have to forsake the important people and concerns of an entire lifetime in order to be satisfied and productive in their later years.

Moreover, with our steadily increasing longevity, all of us in our fifties must continue to produce the income and financial security needed to sustain us while we are in the process of reinvention. Only then will it be possible to provide mature and effective leadership to those organizations and communities about which we most care. Oftentimes this means we must reinvent ourselves in a nonwork context first, rather than beginning the process by dramatically unhooking from our current jobs, tasks, or livelihoods. Indeed, some of us may be attending to our habitual activities with dedication and great caring. There is no need to abandon all meaningful past commitments simply to grow and move forward.

For others of us, however, reinvention will mean making radical changes and taking real risks. We may give up a secure retirement program offered by a long-term employer in order to do new work that is truly more important to us. Or we may take on the role of primary breadwinner, after many years of homemaking or producing a secondary income, perhaps to assist a spouse in shifting to a less demanding work schedule.

While coming to terms with the realities of our lives as fifty-year-old men and women, we need to stop sometimes to listen to our inner voices — those "voices from other rooms," as writer Truman Capote aptly called them[7] — that will help us find our way as we explore our new roles. The renowned Swiss psychoanalyst Carl Jung saw these voices as the undeveloped aspect of ourselves, the part of us that we pushed aside or ignored during the previous decades of our adult lives in order to be practical and realistic. Most of us were willing, then, to fit into our worlds in order to be recognized, rewarded, and accepted. But our increasing years bring us new priorities, and by our fifties, many of us have begun to reconsider our earlier choices.

The process of reinvention in our fifties involves a yearning to become more authentic than we ever allowed ourselves to be before. Those voices from other rooms speak ever more loudly to us now. If we need to silence them, then we are going to have to fill the room in which we live with distractions and endless busyness to drown them out. Such a strategy rarely works, for if the voices are not heard and acknowledged at some point, they have the potential to truly destroy our happiness in our later years. During our fifties, then, we ought to welcome these voices, frightening though they may be. We have reached the stage of life when we have both the time and the wisdom to address their long-ignored concerns.

Conclusions

As each of us begins the second half of his or her personal century, none of us may feel very confident about where decisions made today will lead us. We will have some difficult choices to make among abundant options. In many instances, once meaningful plans and goals, for which we may have worked for years, will need to be discarded. But we can only begin to reinvent ourselves when we have demolished such anchors to a previous time as are no longer serving us. We need to hold on to our useful images at the same time as we replace outmoded images with more nourishing and vitalizing ones. We must realize that the liberation that our reinvention will set into motion is less to be feared than welcomed, because it frees our creative potential for new growth. It lets us find a new vitality and fulfillment inside ourselves, both in relationship to other people and to the world itself.

For some of us this task may seem like a natural progression. For others it may be extraordinarily challenging and require enormous courage. The varied voices and messages of the men and women in this book should help each of us to begin and maintain his or her own process of searching for meaning and growth. We hope that the voices will also speak with eloquence and power to the baby boomers who will soon begin their own journey into their fifties. Their efforts toward reinvention promise to make their fifties decade a profoundly visible one, one that is destined to be, simply by this generation's sheer numbers, the primary driver and arbiter of U.S. values and life-styles for years to come.

2

New Identities,
New Priorities:
Settling Down or Gearing Up?

The first forty years of our lives are spent in developing the text; the second forty in writing the commentary.

—Arthur Schopenhauer

In our discussions with others, we have found two distinct images about being fifty.

"It's Too Late"

The first image was "it's too late," and this negative image was prevalent in a number of the interviews conducted for this book. One fifty-two-year-old woman, for instance, expressed her continuing unhappiness about the effects of her early life upon the rest of her life. She had made a lot of mistakes, she admitted, and she didn't feel she had enough time left to remedy them. She said with resignation, "My life is almost over, and I have already done everything I can to improve my own status or to improve the society in which I live. From this point on, it is up to my children, or at least a younger generation, to correct the ills of this world. It is also too late for me to accomplish what I have wanted in life. I must make do with what I have achieved and acquired."

We can hear the despair, regret, and ultimately stagnation that Erikson tells us this image of life often reflects.[1] For men and women in their fifties who hold this perspective, the central issue really is facing their own mortality. Some, like the woman just described, feel that they have given life their best shot, and it is now up to others to carry on. Some express a fear that to make changes now would lead only to instability. Still others become immobilized by their fear of potential catastrophic illness, isolation, or dependency on others. The major fear of one couple, in which both partners are active and independently employed, is that one of them might become incapacitated. "I've experienced the other end of the stick," the wife related, "when my in-laws came to live with us and lost their ability to care for themselves due to general illnesses and frailty. The prospect of that happening to either one of us really scares me." Another married woman, whose husband is now disabled, confided that it was not aging that was difficult or fearful but rather the possible losses of her own capacities or those of people who were important to her, such as her own children and close friends. Still another couple worried about becoming ill and not having sufficient money to finance the illness, especially if it meant a long convalescence.

As author Roger Gould reminds us, risk-taking can create anxiety and a sense of internal prohibition against proceeding.[2] This is why reinventing ourselves demands a certain courage. From the "it's too late" perspective, the fifties are the beginning of the end.

"Before I Go"

The second major image about being fifty is optimistic and proactive. It might be called, "before I go." Those who expressed this view feel that they have much to do in a short time; therefore, they are rushing to clarify their priorities and redefine their identities. These men and women find that everything still interests them. The things they cared about in their twenties and thirties are still important to them, but these old interests are being supplemented by new interests or by new concerns.

One fifty-year-old man, for instance, is holding onto his dream that he and his wife will move to his mountainside home when he reaches his fifty-fourth birthday, where he will write books and paint. His new fear is that he or his wife might die or become ill before his dream can be fulfilled. There is an urgency in his plan for new beginnings. What is most important, however, is that he is acting on his new interests.

The "before I go" image is coupled with feelings of exhilaration and, in some cases, also with feelings of fatigue. Some people find themselves saying, "I'm too old to be doing all this and to be so interested in so many aspects of life." The central issue for men and women in their fifties who hold a proactive perspective is focusing their currently diffused energies.

Jim is an example of a person with the "before I go" view. At fifty-nine, he is a retired executive from one of the largest corporations in the United States. Soon after his retirement, he left his wife with their home and most of their investments in Philadelphia and moved to California. He has also separated from his children, who are all adults. In his fifties, Jim's need to find new meaning in life became primary. He decided that it was important to be less available to others and to minimize all distractions in order to work on creative projects that he had sacrificed earlier for the sake of supporting and nurturing his family. Jim explains that his voice from another room has been directing him to finish the third draft of his novel, prepare a play he has written for a read through, and begin translating some of the Greek classics. It is important, he feels, to do these things now because he had put aside his creative spirit for the sake of his family when he was a younger man. "I should not have put all my eggs in one basket," he laments, adding, "I can no longer ignore this need to express myself this way. No one in my family understands why I had to move or why I did not meet their expectations of retirement."

Exploring Alternative Identities

To most people, late adolescence still is the most appropriate period of life in which to explore alternative identities and "try out" different roles and experiences. Going to college, joining the military, traveling, or learning a trade as an apprentice or intern are all opportunities for youthful exploration.

There generally has been little tolerance in our society for older men and women who take a "moratorium"[3] or time out from old life-styles in order to try out new identities. Although in the 1990s we are seeing more acceptance of radical life-style changes at a late stage in life, such changes have previously been seen as "out of step with society."[4]

Jim's breaking away from home and family to pursue a career as a writer probably would have been tolerated, although viewed skeptically, by his parents and friends when he was a young man. However, now that he is "grown up," this kind of behavior is judged to be incomprehensible and unacceptable by those who were around him before — even though he has completed his parental responsibilities and shared a long and satisfying marriage with his first wife.

Nevertheless, Jim's actions are a genuine exploration of new sources for giving meaning to his life. One source has proved to be creative expression, which has supplanted the meaning that came from his career involvement with a business corporation and from his family. This is a common change of perspective among fifty-year-olds.

Another source of meaning for Jim is his relationship with a woman who happens to be much younger than his wife. After years of what he calls "passionless dedication" to his first wife, Jim has found someone who shares a new intimacy with him, an intimacy that he had not known previously. The new relationship and his writing are areas of generativity for Jim. Together, they provide him with his "reasons for living."

Reflecting on the vitality his new directions have given him, Jim sees few, if any, impediments to the realization of his creative work. Neither external constraints, such as limited income, nor potential inner vulnerabilities brought about by his isolation from his family seem to matter. "Regardless of any obstacles or how you feel, good or bad," he observes, "you can't give up the things you really like. The reward comes from the inside — from your accomplishments and knowing that what you are doing is good."

At first glance, Jim's life reads like a plot of some run-of-the-mill soap opera entitled "fiftysomething." But for Jim this is real life; he suffers both real pain and real happiness. His voice from another room has not made the choice easy, but it is a voice he knows he must heed.

Jim's story also shows us that when we reinvent ourselves, we are often going to bring others face to face with the need to reinvent themselves. Jim's first wife will also have to learn to grow and develop after many years of involvement with one man and one life-style. What will become of her happiness and life structure? The feeling of "being left behind, after all I've done for you" is more common for women to experience than men, although men too are sometimes left behind. The interviewer did not have the opportunity to find out how Jim's first wife fared, but later in this book we will hear from other women and men who were left behind and had to choose between a continuing life of regret and anger or a new life that required the pain and exhilaration of reinvention.

Men and women play out the divergent images of generativity and stagnation in various ways: either they change, expand, and reorder their priorities; they allow their inner lives to evolve; they revitalize their bodies and minds and develop new myths and images for themselves; or they perform none of these acts of reinvention. Some hold images of endings; others see new beginnings. Most individuals in their fifties, like the man who is preparing to move to his mountain cabin, find themselves planning and creating new identities while keeping important relationships intact and becoming more aware of potential barriers to their new desires. They experience a tension between generativity and stagnation — a tension that is as an integral part of our fifties decade.

Reordering Priorities

We are most likely to feel the tension between generativity and stagnation when we examine our priorities. Once into our fifties, we often feel that the priorities that previously shaped us and seemed so important are undergoing significant or even radical change. To identify how our commitments and activities are changing, we can simply glance at the entries in our daily calendars. Are we seeing certain people much more than we used to? Are we seeing others much less? What new activities are we making time for? What do we no longer seem to be able to find time for? Are last-minute changes entered freely or are entries written in ink and not expected to change?

Some of us who are in our fifties portray this decade as a time of settling down — a time for contemplation and for savoring life's achievements. One fifty-nine-year-old man suggested, for example, that one of the great benefits of this age is having the time to do the things he likes to do: "It is the best time of my life so far. . . . I get to rest and relax when I want to. I like the freedom of doing what I want when I want. It's a wonderful time of life."

Other interviewees, however, projected a less leisurely image. The found their fifties to be a time when many issues pressed and confronted them as never before. The issues were not necessarily new, but the urgency was. Realizing that they have neither an infinite stretch of time nor unlimited energy in front of them, these men and women feel pushed to establish firm priorities, especially as they move closer to their sixties.

One recently remarried man who had just turned sixty had prepared a rather impressive list of high-priority goals that he had hoped to accomplish across the remaining years of his life:

- Stay married forever
- Buy a house
- Have a family
- Pay the doctor bills
- Save money for education
- Be a grandparent

These are not unusual ambitions. Compared to some, they are, in fact, quite modest. What is noteworthy here is that the process of establishing priorities has become salient and urgent.

In another interview, Evelyn, a married woman, described her full and busy life. She spoke about the things that are most important to her and to which she allocates the most time: "I am the mother of four children. I've traveled quite a bit around the world and had wonderful experiences in five countries. I'm also a grandmother of two children. In addition to that, I am a student at [a local graduate school] in the master's program. In fact, I'm in the process of writing my thesis and hope to clear that up [soon]. In addition to being a student, I am also a full-time teacher for the handicapped, and I thoroughly enjoy my job."

Mother, traveler, grandmother, student, and full-time worker—Evelyn is all of these. For this woman and other involved people like her, the multiple, complex roles of adult life require continued priority setting. Such impressive life menus were not uncommon for many of the fifty-year-old men and women we interviewed.

Another interviewee, Pamela, shared a typical daily schedule that begins at 5:30 A.M. with a shower and a half-hour of stretching exercises. She eats breakfast while reading the newspaper and then drives to work. Her work day, commencing at 8:30 each morning, is busy with seeing clients and visiting various health-treatment facilities. She takes a brief break for lunch and completes the afternoon with supervision and management chores. Late in the afternoon, Pamela typically shops for the evening meal, then has dinner with her husband, watches a little television, reads in bed, and finally falls off to sleep about 11:00 P.M.

The lives of many men and women in their fifties are fuller than they have ever been, especially now that young children are no longer underfoot. Another woman, Jean, spoke of the way her priorities had shifted when her children left home: "I don't keep my house as clean as I used to. The grandchildren come and find little dust balls. Some things are just not as important. You're not raising the house, you're raising people. . . . I am still demanding of my own job and production [and have been the] top producer [in my division] for the last two years."

Coming to Grips with What Is Most Important

Our fifties are a time when we typically attend to those things that we most truly care about while allowing other things to remain unattended.[5] One reason for doing this may simply be to survive an onslaught of diverse and pressing demands. If we do not come to grips with what is most important, we face the threat of being overwhelmed by the ever-increasing numbers of people, activities, and demands that often enter our lives in our fifties.

It used to be that our early forties was the time when we typically were confronted with the dual pressures of having aging parents to care for as well as having children making new and greater demands upon us as they pass through the often troublesome ages of late adolescence and early adulthood.[6]

Given that people in the United States now tend to live longer and remain in better health, both physically and mentally, we often will not have to face the increasing dependence of our parents on us until we are well into our fifties or even beyond. Also, given that many men and women are now marrying and having their first children later in life, we can expect more children to reach adolescence when their parents are in their late forties, early fifties, or indeed, even older. Thus, the dual generational demands on what is now being referred to as "the sandwich generation" may be just as likely to occur when we are in our fifties as when we are in our forties.

Demands on us also increase because this is the age at which we are likely to assume positions of leadership in corporations, human service organizations, government agencies, volunteer services, and community groups. The United States is often viewed as a "youth culture," with men and women moving into major positions of leadership in their late thirties and early forties, but the fact remains that the largest proportion of our current leaders have mostly been chosen from those in their fifties and sixties.

Our fifties are also the decade when we are most often acknowledged for our contributions to organizations and to society. Recipients of awards are thought to savor the moment; however, many men and women in their fifties now seem to view recognition as an indication that still more is demanded of their time and talent. They want to contribute more while they are still in a position to make a difference, to be generative and to care for that about which they themselves most deeply care. Indeed, it is this caring that often results in their attaining positions of leadership and achieving recognition.

But where do all these demands lead for men and women in their fifties? Is this a period of crisis and chaos? Or is it a period of excitement and satisfaction at caring for ourselves after a lifetime of caring for others?

From our interviews, we sense that both men and women are finding that they can still choose what is important and try out their identities as never before. One person summarized many of the sentiments expressed by the men and women in our study when he said, "Why can't people see that I am still that arrogant, ambitious, bold, irreverent fool that I was when I was twenty years of age? I have polished this fool a bit and clothed him with establishment clothing and manners. Still, not very far below the surface is that same vital young man — and I am thoroughly enjoying letting it rip and discovering that, now that I am older and a bit more skillful, I can get away with it!"

Gender Differences in Priorities

As men and women come to grips with what is most important to them, gender plays a significant role in the kinds of priorities on which they focus.

The fifty-year-old woman who has primarily led a home-based life may now be ready to be active outside the home, while the fifty-year-old man whose life has been essentially work-based is ready to relax. The woman whose life has been filled with community volunteer activities will often disengage from such organizational commitments. On the other hand, the man will often find time for community-service projects, especially if his work has previously limited his community involvement. In the past, the fifty-year-old man typically had more access than the fifty-year-old woman to leadership roles, both at work and in the community. Now, the woman is finding herself also in demand for these roles.

When Carol Gilligan explored the differences between

men and women in development,[7] she found that the middle years of a woman's life were often a time of return to the unfinished business of adolescence. It is in the adolescent years, says Gilligan, that young women often confuse identity with intimacy, defining themselves through relationships with others. Jean Baker Miller, calling for a new psychology of women, also contends that women develop in a context of attachment and affiliation with others and that their sense of self is organized around their ability to make and maintain affiliations and relationships.[8]

For many women, a broken affiliation is perceived not just as a loss of relationship but as a loss of self. Affiliation, therefore, is often valued by women as highly as (if not more highly than) self-enhancement and individual achievement, which are the prime motivators for most men in our society. Because women's sense of integrity appears to be entwined with an ethic of caring, and because they tend to define themselves through relationships, major transitions in women's lives often involve changes in the way they understand and act out this caring. When women distinguish "between helping and pleasing" and when they free their "activity of taking care" from their wish to have the approval of others, Gilligan believes that their "ethic of responsibility can become a self-chosen anchor of personal integrity and strength,"[9] rather than being something women have because they think they are expected to have it.

Thus, most women reach midlife with a psychological history different from men's and face a different social reality, having had different possibilities for love and for work. However, one of the most interesting aspects of changing, expanding, and reordering priorities in our fifties is that, although the content of the priorities may vary for each gender depending on prior experiences and values, the process of change is the same for both men and women. Moreover, ambiguity and inconsistency are characteristic of this process. The process can also enhance relationships or destroy their very foundations, but, for those we have interviewed, it is unlikely to leave them untouched or unchanged.

The Struggle over Priorities

There are times when being fifty-plus may not feel very positive. Crises seem to pile up, one on top of another, leading one to wonder what happened to the idea of the fifties as the "reclining years" and whether there will ever be a period of quiet and stability. One man we spoke to, for instance, was faced with the death of his father, the marriage of his son, the birth of his first grandchild, a business reversal, the unanticipated failure of his wife to receive a major corporate promotion, the burden of providing and sharing housing with his wife's aging father for five months, and the chore of negotiating with lawyers and accountants concerning the extortion of most of his mother's life savings — all in a single eighteen-month period. Such a sequence of major life-cycle events could hardly be called tranquil.

We learn, however, to balance diverse, life-shaping events — some positive, some negative, some self-initiated, and some outside of our control — from moment to moment. They are often at the heart of our lives during our fifties as we move from one major event to another, finding very little time to worry about the things that have become less important to us. In our struggle over priorities, we live with our generativity. We truly care about those things with which we concern ourselves the most and ignore virtually everything else. (Still, what a relief it would be, just for a minute, if we could be permitted to focus on one single issue!)

Nevertheless, we are aware, as never before, that most things we once thought were critical are not that important. Somehow, things that appear, at first, to be critical find a way of getting solved, healed, and yes, even forgotten. Even though we may be busier, we often find we have considerably more patience.

However, our more reflective perspective, born of age and experience, often makes us recognize that our decisions about the truly important problems and decisions we face are important not just for ourselves but for many other people. As we change our priorities because of our own and others' changing needs, what we do affects our families, our businesses, and indeed, some-times our very societies.

What are some of these changing needs? We must learn to be as wise as Solomon, and perhaps as clever, while negotiating that difficult transition from being a daily parent to our young adult children to simultaneously assuming new parentlike roles for our own aging parents. To our grown children, we are parents who are now advisors, confidants, and, perhaps, friends. And we begin to play these same roles with our own parents. As one of the authors has said, we have become "parents to our parents" while we have become new kinds of parents to our children. This profound relationship transition between two generations, both of which are relying upon us, is not easily accepted or carried out.[10]

As company and organizational leaders, our decisions can and do make a difference to our customers and those who work with and for us. As community leaders who influence the directions taken by community organizations, agencies, or committees, we struggle with difficult choices, balancing our own and society's values, while we try to help solve complex social and economic problems.

As we reframe our lives, the priorities of our marital or significant other relationships will undergo their own metamorphoses. For some, such relationships will be strengthened and new patterns of growth created. For others, the accommodation to new individual priorities may make togetherness more complicated and problematic.

Finally, this concentration on priorities means that we must consciously draw upon our potential for patience and manage our stress. Because we are more physically vulnerable during our fifties, effective stress management is more critical for us during this period of our lives than ever before. We should remember that higher levels of stress can exacerbate addictions and substance abuses such as overeating and alcoholism. These abuses can be difficult to overcome during this period of our life because many of us are much less attracted to abstinence and denial than when we were younger.

Confronting the Dream

The complex pressures associated with demanding and diverse priorities can cause a crisis of values. As was described earlier, there is a real urgency for many people in their fifties to decide what is truly important for them. Men, in particular, must confront the fact that the dream that they crafted in their twenties concerning career, family, fame, and success is either not going to be realized, has already been realized but isn't as great as they thought it would be, or has been realized and is now no longer a source of guidance for their future lives.[11] For many women, their fifties represent times of dream-reassessment and catching-up. Middle-class women whose dreams were put aside because of childrearing responsibilities or whose dreams were never fully identified in their youth may see their fifties as their one last chance to both create and achieve their dreams.

However they confront their dreams, both men and women in their fifties are faced with the loss of many of the aspirations that they held in abeyance for many years. Often these aspirations date back to when they were twenty or thirty and chose to move in one direction and not in another in regard to career, family, or life-style. Now they discover that they must choose to fulfill only a few parts of their original dreams, or they must recognize that by choosing to do many things, they may not be as successful in completing them.

Support for the Reordering Process

In our fifties, most of us choose to focus on fewer and higher priorities, and this makes it essential that we reorder our values. We also need to identify supportive structures and relationships through which we can grieve for the loss of the values and aspirations we are setting aside and shall probably never again address.

Such support can be found in many settings. Our wives, husbands, and significant others are all invaluable at this point. They can become an important source of support and under-

standing in ways that previously were unknown to either partner. For one couple who has been married thirty-one years and
has eight children, the first half of the marriage was what the
wife considered to be a traditional one, in which she was responsible for childrearing, housework, finances, scheduling appointments, and entertaining guests. As the children grew older the
marriage entered a turbulent phase. She filed for divorce on three
occasions and began dating others, but soon realized the men
she was attracted to were actually similar to her husband. "I
[finally] decided I'd rather be with the father of my children,"
she remembered. "Besides, [my husband and I] have a whole
lot of history." Now they share many household duties, and their
relationship has grown more intimate. Says the wife of her husband, "He has a great sense of humor. One morning I asked
him 'to put a head' on my cup of coffee. He went right over
to my coffee cup and put his head right on it! I came to realize
that an important part of marriage is remembering to be nice
to each other and not to take each other for granted." As a gesture
of mutual affection, each of them puts sentimental notes in odd
places for the other to find and enjoy.

Our children can also begin to return the kind of caring
support we gave to them over many years. Adult children often
become best friends to their parents during their fifties. A friend
of one of the authors, for example, recently went through a
difficult divorce during his early fifties. One of his most important sources of support during this difficult transition was his
two children. He stayed with his daughter for several weeks and
found her insights and comfort to be extraordinary and unanticipated. His son came to live with him while training for a
new job. A new level of friendship and camaraderie emerged
as the two of them spent many evenings talking late into the
night. While the absence of his ex-wife was painful, this man
found that his son and daughter helped to fill the void in a manner that would never have been possible when he and they were
younger.

Other common sources of support are good friends, peers,
self-help groups, and individual and group psychotherapy. Community activity groups, and groups of friends from work and

the neighborhood become as significant for what they can give to those in their fifties as for what the participants can give to the groups and their causes.

The Search for Integrity

As we change, expand, and reorder our priorities, we require a new clarity in our perception of self. In our fifties we need to decide what we truly care about and then start caring about those things more deeply. To do so requires more than a casual, perfunctory decision. Rather, each of us must take time to become quiet and still in order to reflect on our lives and the meaning of our past decisions. Our attention needs to shift from those things that we do best to those things that we most want to do. We must become less expedient and more values-oriented in our actions and behavior. We must learn to focus in order to make the best use of our limited energy and time.

It is now time to look seriously at our actions and our words and make them congruent with each other. Either we change our actions to make them conform to our words — not an easy task when the actions have a long history and are habitual — or we change our words to make them more compatible with what we can and will do in our lives.

For many men and women, their fifties are an era in which their words can truly be trusted; they do exactly what they say they are going to do. They realize that there is no longer time left in their lives to be less than honest and frank with themselves and with those they care about. The veils of pleasing and accommodation fall. Game playing and half-truths are put aside. Individuals start being true to who and what they basically are. Those who face the death of their parents in this period of development may discover that this loss is also a significant psychological turning point, one that empowers the adult son or daughter to be more honest — to reclaim that all-powerfulness which the child once believed resided only in the parents. Mortality unlocks that door. An extraordinary consciousness shift enables us to take that power into ourselves, to find our own unique voices and to become ever more complete and whole.

Inevitably, such developments and changes lead us to a deeper integrity of self. Finding this completeness is one of the most important — yet often unacknowledged — developmental phenomena through which many of us will move during our fifties. Integrating thought, word, and deed begins this major developmental task.

Moral Challenges

Our fifties are the years when both men and women are most capable of exhibiting a morality of mutual care, a care that is no longer simply duty but the result of growing integrity.[12] When we possess mutual care, we care about ourselves and about others. Our decisions tend to be compatible with our moral principles and are tempered by the specific situations in which we find ourselves. We are inclined to act as well as speak in a manner that is sensitive to the people about whom we truly care. Furthermore, our actions are more likely to be compatible with our beliefs about universal justice and equity. We support the individual rights of all men and women, including ourselves, while acknowledging, through word and action, our collective responsibility for other members of our society and other societies — past, present, and future.

We are usually required to and are capable of meeting these moral challenges during our fifties. The changing, expanding, and reordering process of reflection and action is the primary tool with which we achieve the real goal — finding integrity in our lives. This struggle for integrity is the growth edge of our personal process of reinvention in our fifties.

3

Stories and Dreams:
Listening to Inner Voices

> We are our stories and our dreams.
> —*Robert Shukraft*

When people in our society enter their fifties, they are likely to become more attentive to their inner lives than they were at any earlier age. In addition, they report spending more time reflecting on their past. Their orientation shifts from the rich tapestry of future aspirations to an equally rich tapestry of past memories that encapsulate vital emotions such as pain, sorrow, or happiness and vivid details of an original experience — memories that are our own version of "virtual reality."

Memories and Priorities

Our memories can be used in quite different ways during our fifties, some positive and some negative.

The negative side is that these memories can become vehicles for escape and avoidance when we retreat into them and live within them. We cease to create the new experiences and, consequently, the new memories that prevent us from stagnating. We avoid the creation of new dreams about the future; instead, we live almost exclusively with images of the past. Such stagnation is closely related to remorse and regret. We dwell on what could have been or might have been and spend the rest of our lives looking backward in time rather than forward.

On the positive side, memories can provide reassurance and sustenance during difficult times so that we can remain vital and alive during our fifties despite hardships, losses, and disappointments. Other positive aspects are the lessons to be learned from our memories. What exactly is it that we remember? When we reflect upon the events we remember well and try to recapture those that are dim, then we are likely to be provided with clues as to what is really important to us.

For all three of the authors, for instance, the details that occupied our earlier years about what it was we really did in any one organization or school, or about the various reactions to the work we completed, tend to fade away. What we remember most clearly now are the special relationships we formed with the men and women with whom we worked. We remember the personal, thoughtful, and often intimate conversations with a wide variety of wonderful people, perhaps over a meal, or on a walk through a forest, or along a beach. We remember less of what we talked about that had to do with our work, but more of the personal statements that each of us shared. We remember, especially, how those conversations led to deep and lasting relationships and to our own personal development.

We remember the trips to conferences and to distant consultations. One of us remembers the beautiful yellow aspen trees in a canyon he drove through on a fall afternoon while traveling to a college in Utah. Not much is remembered about what happened at this college, except for the occasional use of silver dollars to pay the college staff in an effort to demonstrate the importance of such coins to the local economy. One of us remembers flying into Washington, D.C., and being moved by the monuments and renewed sense of history, even after twenty years of work in the capital. What special reasons were there for our numerous trips? There were many surely, but we hardly remember what they were.

Given the large number of alternative things men and women in their fifties can do—"tending our overgrown garden," we like to call it—they often look to the memories that remain clear from their past as signposts toward what might truly become the most important priorities for their fifties. Memories, thus, can be catalysts for generativity. When misused, they can become excuses for stagnation. All of us have a choice.

Storytelling

As the chapter-opening quote from Robert Shukraft states, our stories and our dreams are what define our inner selves.[1] In their fifties, men and women look more closely at the stories of their lives. They ask, Where am I in my career? What difference have I made in the life of my family? Among my friends? In the community? In society? No longer can they look only at their dreams of the future for reassurance about their worth in the world. Instead, with increasing frequency, they look back to see what they have already accomplished and what values are exemplified in the critical decisions they have already made.

As we all take stock of our past lives, somehow we must find meaning in them. If we do not, then we at least must find some source of understanding, or even self-forgiveness, for actions that we have taken and that can never be undone.

Gwen, one of the women in our study, revealed that her greatest failures have centered around "not being able to see the long term of things. Getting too engrossed in the difficulties of the moment and thinking that things are never going to be any different than they are at the moment. It's a difficult time, as though there is no tomorrow. Looking back on earlier times, I can see that if I had been able to step back only a little bit, I could have realized what things were going on — things I knew intellectually but wasn't able to apply when I should have." Gwen compared her own impatience to that of her father's. She stated her firm commitment to being somehow different from her stubborn and often bitter dad, as she herself comes to terms with the second half of her life.

For Gwen and for many of the men and women we interviewed, the image of a significant person in their past (often a father or mother) becomes especially powerful as they enter their fifties. The lives of those from their past often speak forc-

ibly to them about what they should or should not do, as Gwen's
memories of her father came back to set a clear example of how
not to lead the second half of her life.

Listening to Voices from Other Rooms

These images from the past are like Truman Capote's "voices
from other rooms." Fifty-year-old men and women begin to listen
to these voices in order to attend to those parts of themselves
that they abandoned earlier in their lives. One man who gave
up the theater as a "childish" and "unrealistic" pursuit in his early
twenties now returns to community theater. A woman who loved
reading literature when she was young finds time again to pick
up and reread the classics of her childhood with new insights.
Some return to fishing or baseball, others to movies or sewing,
to dancing or playing cards, or simply to enjoying "doing nothing" — activities that they had left behind when they assumed
the heavy burdens of young adulthood.

Fred is a fifty-year-old man who came to the United States
from England when he was twenty-six. He had always wanted
to go to sea, and as a young man, he had dreamed of going
to a maritime academy or studying naval law, but instead chose
a more "practical" career in a machine tools trade that would
pay well and provide security. Recently, Fred's "impractical"
voice became more persistent. When Fred received an invitation to go to Hawaii and to return to the U.S. mainland by naval
vessel, it seemed to be a dream come true. He accepted the invitation readily. While driving to the airport, he reminisced,
"When I was driving to the airport, knowing that I was going
to be getting on an airplane and flying to Hawaii to join this
ship and then sailing back, [it was] a very, very happy day for
me. I had a hard time realizing it was happening and was excited when I realized I was on my way. It was really a thrill
for me."

Many different "voices from other rooms" can speak to
us in our fifties. They can be disturbing voices when they suggest that our old behaviors and priorities are no longer compatible with the things we truly value now. While Charles Dick-

ens's Scrooge may have had to wait for Christmas to awaken voices from his past, men and women in their fifties are likely to hear such voices at any time. Such voices provide guidance and sometimes contradict the voices men and women hear from society and even from those close to them — their wives, husbands, children, best friends, or lovers.

Changing Attitudes

When we reach our fifties, some of our most basic attitudes can change. For example, like many of the people we interviewed, Gwen (the woman who regretted learning impatience from her father) spoke of becoming less opinionated about things once she entered her fifties. The interviewees often said they had a greater tolerance for other people and cultures, as well as a fuller appreciation for the life-styles of the younger generation than ever before. This newfound tolerance may be partly a function of the "graduation" of many of us from active parenting. We are likely to be more tolerant of people whom we don't have to live with every day. It may also result from a growing sense of assurance about our own accomplishments and wisdom. Gwen, for instance, feels that she has become less opinionated because she is now more successful in her career: "I've learned how to work with people and pick out a part and do something and not get involved with the politics."

Making our actions more consistent with our espoused values also requires us to change our attitudes. One of the authors' fifty-year-old colleagues recently spoke of the ways in which he has simplified his life in order to make his behavior more congruent with his values: "I devote myself to three things: my children [twins born when I was in my forties], my wife, and my career. I have no time for, and little interest in, other things." He devotes himself to keeping healthy, making money, and nurturing a handful of very important relationships. His life is now highly organized around these few priorities. What is important now is that he continue to listen to the voices from other rooms so that as his values continue to evolve (and his career and children mature) he can continue to live consistently with his values.

Thinking in Contexts

We now know that as both men and women grow older they become more likely to think about values and make moral decisions within the contexts of specific relationships and specific settings, rather than in some general, abstract sense. Mary Field Belenky and her colleagues described this behavior for women.[2]

Our study suggests that men in their fifties also tend to be guided by a sense of the immediate context in which they find themselves. Perhaps this is why our society often describes older men as less decisive and less predictable than younger men. Some observers have noted that this shift inward enables men to be more sensitive and intuitive, more "like women" in their thinking and valuing as they grow older.

We have seen that men and women in their fifties are increasingly likely to translate their words into congruent actions. In their efforts to consider the context of events, they are also more likely to look at other people's actions, rather than merely pay attention to their words. Thus, they listen more, they say less, and they make fewer commitments in order to be sure of keeping them. They also expect other people to keep their commitments. This can contribute to the labeling that sometimes occurs of men and women of this age group as more "introverted," "conservative," or "critical" than younger adults.

Our Male and Female Guides

Jung found that men and women in their fifties are particularly likely to explore those formerly discounted aspects of themselves that are frequently associated with the opposite sex.[3]

In *The Aeneid,* the sibyl, or prophetess, guides Aeneas on his journey through the underworld. In *The Divine Comedy,* Beatrice accompanies Dante in his passage through hell and ascent into Paradise. Such mythical and literary guides have counterparts in real life. Many men seem to begin their in-depth exploration of their "feminine" potentialities with the help of a woman who becomes their guide. She often is not the woman to whom they are married — although she can be. A man's turning to another woman for insight and support is often interpreted by his wife or significant other as a betrayal. The other woman may be perceived as a threatening rival, even though the relationship is usually not a sexual one.

The female guide may be someone involved in spiritual work, or someone who is several years older than the male. She may be a valued colleague with whom a man has worked for years or a neighbor who is engaged in creative pursuits. Their relationship typically becomes richer and more personal over a period of five or ten years. The man becomes intrigued with her work and life, and while this relationship may be felt by the man as "true love" or "real intimacy," it is usually foolhardy for him to give up his existing relationship for this woman. She needs, rather, to stay at some distance and serve as the man's guide to his *anima*, the female spirit or energy force that Jung says is found in every male.

The anima's role is to deliver a man into a consciousness that is based on empathetic participation in life, not on heroic self-mastery. When heroic consciousness dominates, one thinks that one knows better than one's unconsciousness who one is. Do men turn to such female guides because of their inability to know their own anima as an inner guide? Such a notion seems entirely plausible.

Yet other men in their fifties seek the counsel of another man, someone with more life experience, understanding, or wisdom. These more mature male guides can also become the guide who enables younger men to explore their inner feelings and reflections and to come to grips with their other voices. Men in their fifties, thus, might do well to find an appropriate female or male mentor to help guide them toward a better understanding of their own personal underworld, or unconscious.

Similarly, many women find men other than their husbands — or they find "wise" women — to serve as guides to their *animus*, the male spirit or energy force found in every female. Just as a wife is suspicious of her husband's female guide, a husband is likely to view his wife's male guide as an undesirable intrusion into their domestic life. This male guide is sometimes a colleague at work; more often, however, he comes from another part of the woman's life. The animus guide may even be quite romantic and attentive, exhibiting some of the old-fashioned virtues of male chivalry. Like the male's female guide, the male guide is rarely a satisfactory potential spouse. He is of much greater value when serving the woman at a distance, allowing the romance and introspection to build rather than being dissipated by an actual sexual encounter.

This Jungian view helps to explain why new and strong relationships occur between men and women in their fifties. It also provides us with a yellow caution light when and if a spouse appears to be involved in a marriage-threatening relationship. Although it may be difficult to distinguish between a "guide" and a sexual competitor, it is important for both men and women to understand these dynamics and to resist the temptation to draw premature conclusions about a spouse's psychologically intimate relationship.

Finding Sanctuaries

Men and women in their fifties also often look to special places, or sanctuaries, in which to reflect on and renew their inner lives. Robert Johnson calls these sanctuaries "Grail Castles," after the legendary heroes whose search for the Holy Grail was a great pilgrimage to fulfill their being and to make them whole.[4] Such a special place, especially for men, may often be located in the woods or by a body of water. Typically, it is a setting that differs radically from the setting of their work or family.

These excursions to hike in the woods, climb, hunt, or fish are not primarily a matter of catching or killing anything but rather of filling men's needs to find special places where they can be alone and do much of their reflection. They may take their anima guide to this special spot, or at least talk with her about their Grail Castle (real or imagined). One qualification for an effective anima guide is that she be willing to listen patiently and sympathetically to extended monologues about the man's Grail Castle and the inner striving he does there.

Some men may also explore their inner spiritual life at a retreat site, or even at their local church, participating in a variety of church-related activities that provide them with what they call an "excuse to be alone" with their thoughts and feelings in a setting conducive to spiritual growth. However, men sometimes sabotage their introspective efforts by letting their sanctuary, or Grail Castle, itself become a distraction. They may spend their time chopping wood at the cabin or become immersed in the politics of their church.

During the last few years, Tom, now in his midfifties, takes time away from his family each year to participate in a one-week retreat in the Southern California mountains. "It's my time to be alone," he admits. "Being in nature like that really is special. It's a time to think and to do some planning. No telephones, no kids interrupting. I really have a chance to get to know who I really am. It's such a busy schedule between work and the kids, I never get time to think like that when I'm home. Jane [his wife] really doesn't mind me taking the time away, for I try to let her have her own time whenever she feels she needs it." For Tom, and others like him, such "time away" creates a regenerative atmosphere for new growth.

Similarly, many women who are in their fifties identify special places which give them opportunities for introspection and inner search. For many women, these sanctuaries may often be found in their own homes. The sister of one of the authors, for example, has designated an area of her large kitchen, complete with filing cabinet, desk area, and computer, as her private preserve. Another friend has made a small second-story bedroom in her home into her "off-limits" hideaway in which to think, write, and create. Still other women may look not to the home but to some cottage hideaway in the woods as their special place. Virginia Woolf said that women need a "room of their own" in order to find the intellectual freedom to be creative artists.[5] However, it seems that many women in their fifties want their own rooms in which to do their inner work, whether it is artistic or not.

For many women, a sanctuary is much more a state of mind than it is for men. They care less about what their special place looks like than they do about being alone in a place that is truly their own. If a woman has an animus guide, he will be wise not to intrude into this special time or place unless invited.

The actual work that men and women in their fifties do

in their sanctuaries may not be as important as the opportunities these hideaways give them to think and to be "inside their
own heads." Men and women who do not have sanctuaries into
which to retreat may miss the chance to find their inner selves,
or become angry and impatient with others who crowd their
space, yet not be able to explain just why they feel frustrated.

A Few Special Relationships

Men and women in their fifties need not only special places and
times for introspection but also a few special relationships, in
addition to their anima or animus guides. Typically, the number and variety of our relationships diminishes as we enter our
fifties. Most of us tend to keep a few close friends, allowing the
others to "go gently into the night." The friends we hold on to
tend to be those with whom we can truly reflect upon our inner
life. In our fifties, our friends are less likely to be business associates. Instead, they may be friends from childhood or another
passage of life. They may be from our church, our jogging
group, our intimate social world, or even our neighborhood.
They are definitely not let's-do-lunch-someday types of friends.

New forms of intimacy, openness, and candor are now
explored. We discover we can form close friendships with people of the opposite sex without having to "play games" or fend
off misguided sexual advances. In the best of worlds, we find
our anima or animus guide among our cherished friends.

Even more important at this point in our lives, each of
us should find one new special friend — ourselves. We should
learn to both comfort and support ourselves. If we remain dis-
engaged from ourselves, especially from those parts of our identities that we have disowned for many years, then we will never
succeed at "the final development task" of our lives: namely, the
integration of our disparate elements into a unified and coherent sense of self.[6] Underneath all our other motives, it is this
search for complete integration that motivates us toward reex-
ploration and reinvention in our fifties and focuses much of our
private energy on coming to terms with ourselves.

There is an irony here. Just at the time when our external career and community lives are becoming most visible and

we increasingly find ourselves in public leadership positions, our internal search for meaning is also emerging as a priority. And it must remain a priority. Both our own and others' expectations of us demand clarity of vision. Our internal struggle to clear away the inner clouds and to affirm, both for ourselves and for others, the worthiness of our lives is at the center of our quest for integration in our fifties.

Spirituality: Is There a Quest?

Does our attention to our inner lives in our fifties produce some greater development of spirituality? The responses of our seventy-three men and women indicate that the spiritual path for fifties men and women continues to be individual and personal, more often translated into a code of ethics about living than into a philosophical, religious, or spiritual quest.

One fifty-four-year-old, a very creative housewife and mother, when asked about her spiritual perspective, shared how her fundamentalist Baptist grandmother had influenced her. The main influence, however, was not toward her grandmother's religion. Instead, like her grandmother, she had gradually become more tolerant and accepting of other people's belief systems, despising narrowness and bigotry and practicing tolerance. She doesn't associate herself with any particular denomination today, she admitted, but she does believe in God and tries to live by the Golden Rule.

Judy, a fifty-seven-year-old working woman with three grown children, has been married to the same man for almost forty years. Her husband, who is now preparing for retirement, is almost one year older than she. Born in 1929, they were both raised with the belief that, when it comes to morals, things are either right or wrong. But Judy confesses that "I now see more gray than I think my husband does. I can't say he is a redneck because that is not right, but he is very vocal about something being right and something being wrong, and that there's no in between." Translating her ethics into religion and churchgoing, she noted, "We both were baptized—but we don't go regularly." She paused a moment while she reflected and then said, "I believe in some sort of a power. I think we both believe in the

Ten Commandments, to a degree. I think we practice what we preach. We do unto others as we'd like done unto ourselves. But we don't go to church regularly."

Many of those we interviewed seem to hold thoughts that revealed a return to or continuation of earlier practices and beliefs in applying religious lessons to the tasks of daily living and relating to others.

Arnold, a respected fifty-one-year-old art and antique dealer, was born in Salt Lake City of a Mennonite artist father and a Mormon housewife mother. He is a contented man who represents an interesting bundle of opposites: deeply spiritual, but antireligious; contemplative but anti-intellectual; radical in contrast to his conservative upbringing, yet conservative in contrast to his counterculture adulthood when, in his late twenties, he left Utah for "the purple hills of hippiedom in San Francisco" and met his future wife.

"Salvation and enlightenment are something that exist at all times," he remarked when asked to describe his own spirituality. "We just have to wake up to it. Like grace, it's something that you can't force into awareness through discipline. Instead, it just might hit you on the head, regardless of your good works. Be as good as you can and hope for the best." He paused for a moment, as if he wasn't quite sure where to go with these thoughts and then concluded, "There is probably no necessary connection between these two injunctions!"

Some people are able to accept various aspects of spirituality without thinking deeply about them. Others find spirituality through life experiences that leave a profound impact. Death, perhaps of a parent or significant other, can be a powerful reflection of one's own mortality. One fifty-seven-year-old woman, Anne, who recently separated from her husband for the second time and is the mother of three grown sons, is trying to come to terms with her life. Part of her new personal fulfillment comes from the part-time work she does with two hospices. She spoke movingly about her work with the dying:

> When you work with death, you begin to see "deathing as birthing" — as a transition. . . . When you begin to think of death, you start to realize how much

pain there has been, and when you see people struggle as they do, your values change. Little things
aren't important anymore. . . . You start to say,
"Where do things fit in the larger scheme of things?"
But you do it without paying attention to detail.
I don't mean . . . that you let everything go by because it doesn't matter in the bigger scheme, but
you value the person who does care enough to say,
"Hi! How are you?" You value the hug that's spon-
taneous and real.

Fifty-year-old men and women who have been emotionally and
psychologically touched by death often experience a shift in consciousness and a new way of seeing the world. As Anne says,
"Your values change."

Confronting Death

Over the last few years, one of the authors of this book has had
to deal with the deaths of more than thirteen of his closest friends
from diseases related to the AIDS epidemic, as well as his own
mother's death and the death of one of his mentors. All of these
events have had a powerful impact on his life. At age fifty-three,
he found his own spiritual journey quickening and becoming
deeper. Brought up in the Episcopal faith, he spent a number
of his formative years while working abroad studying and experiencing South Asian and Middle Eastern religions. He views
India as his spiritual home and sees himself as being more
spiritual than religious. The wisdom gained in those years is
helping him now in his fifties as he copes with the issues of separation and the meaning and significance of death itself.

He finds himself placing friendship even higher than before on his changing list of values, being less concerned with
accomplishments, more focused on the quality and richness of
life itself, and continually sorting out and discarding or ignoring the unimportant. In the decade of his fifties, he has come
to realize that, since death cannot be avoided, the real question
becomes, "How shall we live?" Ironically, it is death that keeps
him honest about life.

4

Body and Mind:
Over the Hill
or In Our Prime?

Forty is the old age of youth. Fifty is the youth of old age.
—Anonymous

One of the images about being fifty that worries many men and women depicts the deterioration of body and mind that is supposed to occur during this decade. Fifty-year-old men and women often respond to this image by making conscious decisions about the ways in which they will use their bodies and minds, not only during this decade but throughout the rest of their lives. Our interviews focused on three areas of body and mind: physical health, sexuality, and learning and education.

Concerns About Physical Health

In our fifties our basic physical strength is unimpaired. We can still lift and carry pretty much what we did when we were younger. On the other hand, we can't do physical things as many times in a specific time interval as we used to. Our stamina is not as great. Our recuperative powers have declined.

One of the men we interviewed recalled when he and his father (then in his late seventies) had an arm-wrestling bout some ten years ago: "I was very surprised to find that he held his own and was still a very strong man. We held each other to a draw.

I suspect, however, that he could not have repeated the feat one hour later and would not have been able to hold his own the second or third time that we arm-wrestled together. Similarly, at this point in my life, I could probably hold my twenty-one-year-old son to a draw but probably couldn't defeat him with repeated engagements."

But have we lost as much stamina as we often think we have, or is our loss of physical strength and stamina a self-fulfilling and untested assumption based on our expectations about growing older and losing vitality? We are influenced so much by our myths and images. Do we plod upstairs slowly because of the myth or because we actually have a little less endurance than we did before? One of our interviewees said, "I am waiting for the first time when someone on a crowded bus offers me a seat, rather than my offering a seat, as I now often do, to someone who is older than myself. When do I begin to believe that I am growing old and when does the aging process become a reality? When do I become 'the old person' who deserves a seat on the bus?"

Keeping Trim and Fit

The men and women we interviewed seem either obsessively concerned with health, exercise, and diet or "defiantly" resistant to these concerns. One of the men, Charlie, considers a "red letter day" for him to be one in which he is able to accomplish many physical feats: he runs twelve miles, does push-ups, gets his body in shape, and then relaxes.

Two fifty-year-old male colleagues are obsessed about their diets. They talk almost nonstop about what they are eating that is healthy, what they have stopped eating that is unhealthy, and what everyone around them should be eating in order to remain or get healthy. "Unhealthy" food has become their adversary. While both men successfully battled with organizations in their thirties and forties, they now, in their fifties, battle themselves to rid their bodies of "evil toxins" and "bad cholesterol." They, like many fifty-year-olds have opted for youthful vigor as a priority, helping to swing the pendulum of our culture more and more to healthy living.

Concerns for diet and weight were even more common among women with whom we talked. When asked about her biggest failure up to this point in her life, Donella immediately pointed out that it was the many diets she'd been on: "I am constantly trying to lose weight, and I consider it a failure since I'm still overweight and I'm still struggling with the problem. So when I think of all the things that have happened to me in my life, I think this would be my greatest failure. At the same time, it's something that's still ongoing, and I continue to work at it."

Another midfifties woman, Brenda, a wife and mother, similarly considers her "round and overweight body" to be her major failure in life: "I would have liked to have better genes and to have been born tall and thin. I would have liked to have remained thin. . . . My failure is fighting my weight up and down, up and down." Brenda talked about the societal pressures on girls and women to fit into the thin and perfectly proportioned ideal of female beauty in the United States. When asked how such pressures affected her, she said she had never doubted her intellectual capacity, but she did feel terribly inferior because she did not match the ideal slender, all-American, cheerleader body type. She continues to be preoccupied with dieting and food preparation and describes the physical frustration and insecurity she feels as a result of her negative body image.

One of the authors, attempting to heal a back ailment stemming from the corporate stress with which he was then coping in his early fifties, entered a jazz dance class as its oldest student in order to stretch and strengthen his back muscles (which other approaches had failed to do) as well as to provide some outlet in his limited busy schedule for his creative energies. Not only was the back problem corrected but he has enjoyed staying on as one of the more active and long-term members of the group. He views the workout as revitalizing and healthy and as a tremendous focusing technique that he has learned to carry into his daily routine.

Like many others in their fifties, such men and women seem to have joined a growing number of mature adults intent on taking better care of themselves through diet and exercise and practicing an evolving philosophy of integrating body, mind, and spirit. Not everyone in this age group, however, has joined the health and fitness club. Whether it is due to the lack of time, concern, or simply out of habit, many continue to pursue a lifestyle that soon may seem more appropriate for an earlier era. The pattern for the moment, however, is decidedly mixed.

Sexuality and Fulfillment

Many men and women experience an elevated sexual interest during their fifties — an interest that they frequently enjoy but that society in general has not yet accepted.

In addition, however, sexual pleasure for both men and women in their fifties usually involves adapting to some physical changes. For men, the frequency of orgasm, the ease of erection, the intense and forceful ejaculations, and the relatively short refractory period that marked their earlier sexual life may now all decrease as they experience a reduction in androgen and testosterone levels. However, for most men, this process is gradual and protracted, so that a man's reaction to the changes depends largely on how secure he is within himself, on the extent to which his self-esteem is sexualized in a macho fashion (so that, for example, he considers frequency of orgasm to be the most important measure of his sexuality), and on whether he can acknowledge his own developing "feminine" needs for tenderness and nurturing, which are typically emerging in this period of his life.[1]

For women, the end of menstruation often brings with it a new sense of well-being as they stop experiencing the fluctuating hormone levels that may have been affecting their sexual lives. Also, now that she has no fear of pregnancy, a woman's lustier fantasies can be played out, if she wishes, without inhibitions. This can mean that fifty-year-old men's and women's sexual interests become more closely matched.[2]

When Beth was asked at the end of her interview if there was anything else she wanted to say about herself, there was a long hesitation before she added that she did want to talk about her relationship with her husband, saying, "When I said I really care about my husband and have strong feelings, I feel that being this age has changed my biological and sexual needs, and that my husband and I get along so much better. I said to him I hope it isn't just because I'm fifty, or whenever women are supposed to have their sexual peak, but I do feel more, uh, more sexual. And I am enjoying sex more than I ever did."

Such newfound enjoyment in sex is certainly not exclusive to women. While middle-age men do not, as far as we know, experience the same biologically based new lease on life that postmenopausal women so often enjoy, our interview data indicates that, for whatever reason, a number of men seem as revitalized as their wives. Their sexual lives have been reenergized and even heightened. As Barry, a midfifties colleague of one of the authors remarks, "I thought that things would calm down when I got a bit older, but I find the women just as attractive as ever. Now the older women are looking wonderful! Every one of them is now in my range. And I seem to be more attractive to women than I've ever been. It's great, but not always easy for me or my wife!"

Other men whom we interviewed concur that this is a rich but difficult time of life. Barry's wife is naturally upset about his possible or real philandering, and the dilemma faced by Barry as he finds it more difficult to stay within marital bounds seem to apply to both the men and women in our study. Many women also find these years to be sources of both great sexual fulfillment and reduced marital tension. Freed from fears of pregnancy and the restraints of birth control, they are enjoying themselves more in their lovemaking and seem less fearful of their sexual selves. The candor about women's sexuality encouraged by the feminist movement is starting to seem appropriate for them personally. Men and women whose children are finally out of the house also discover that their newfound privacy is conducive to more frequent and expressive sexuality.

Society's attitudes toward this new sexuality are less open. Men remain fertile well into old age, but a man in his fifties, or older, whose partner gives birth to a child is thought to be beyond the acceptable era of fatherhood. A man in his fifties who is sexually attracted to women younger than he may well be labeled "a dirty old man," while women in their fifties are sometimes gently reminded of their age and place when attracted to any man, especially a younger man. Part of the problem is that societal norms have not yet caught up to actual behavior. There are no clear societal images of what men or women should be like or act like in their fifties, yet clearly, the image of men and women preparing for old age in their fifties is outmoded.

We believe that a realistic sexual image for men and women in their fifties should address the continuing strength of the sexual drive in both sexes. Although fifty-year-olds may have fewer orgasms than they used to, the sex drive for men and women in their fifties certainly appears to be as strong as it is for younger men and women, while the sexual experiences reported by the people we interviewed often seemed to be far more satisfying than at any earlier time in their lives.

Second, we believe that the sexuality of many men and women in their fifties is closely tied to a newfound and deeper quality of intimacy. Men and women report more patience in their sexuality. They savor the experience as well as the outcome. The physical and emotional setting becomes infinitely more important to them. Men and women both seem to become more romantic and to look forward to being in special places that enhance their lovemaking.

Third, the new sexual image should recognize that older people frequently think of themselves as having young bodies. Many of the people we interviewed spoke of the incongruity they perceived between the body they saw every morning in the mirror and the body that they experienced internally when making love. "I simply do not feel as old as I look!" was a common comment. Some of the men and women interviewed overestimated their physical stamina and were surprised by the fatigue they sometimes felt after vigorous lovemaking because it didn't go with their "young" bodies. Passion is certainly there, but there may not always be the energy to fully explore and dissipate this passion. The feeling of being in a young body is sometimes a source of frustration as well as a source of gratification. However, these men and women also talk about savoring a "leftover passion" that seems to confirm for them that they are still very alive and very vital.

We found that the sexual fantasies of men and women in their fifties are also different from those of their youth. Men and women spoke of having fantasies involving their personal sexual past, whereas the fantasies of their youth were of making love with some idealized person they had never met. Thus, a man in his fifties may fantasize about his wife when she was younger rather than fantasizing about some unobtainable Rita Hayworth or Playboy bunny–type as he once did. Similarly, a woman of comparable age might fantasize about a past boyfriend or lover in a particularly romantic setting rather than about some handsome leading man or some stranger she might have met at work years ago. Much younger men and women, remembered either from an earlier time or the present time as well as men and women in their forties or fifties, now become acceptable fantasy lovers.

A final issue, and an important one for those of us in our fifties, concerns the sexuality of our own parents. We now remember our parents when they were in their fifties and come to a startling recognition: "My parents must have been sexual beings! They, too, must have felt like young kids in old folks' skins!" A new sensitivity towards one's parents often emerges from this recognition, and some people in our study talked about being less sexually inhibited around their own children as a result of it. We are at a time when we can more fully recognize and appreciate our own sexuality and its continuity with past and future generations.

"This Menopause Stuff"

For women, the onset of menopause is an undeniable reminder that our bodies are in fact growing older and changing. This biological passage covers a span of five to seven years, usually starting around forty-seven or forty-eight and extending into the midfifties. There are no clear-cut cues as to when this transition actually begins or ends. It is not a sudden event but takes place gradually, as estrogen and other hormone production slows down until the ovaries finally stop putting out much estrogen at all. For some American women, symptoms of menopause seem to be occurring earlier than in the recent past, sometimes becoming evident as early as the late thirties.

Although most women have started through the menopause by the time they reach fifty, their sexual magic is certainly not finished. The transition is so unique for each woman that no clear definition of what does happen and what should happen has yet been formed. For some it may be a time when they need much support from those close to them and from medical science.

Brenda, for example, one of the few women in our study to speak frankly about menopause, had a very difficult time and referred to this physical "given" as "most important" in her life. While acknowledging that not every woman experiences the extent of discomfort that she is experiencing, she finds that her symptoms include migraine headaches, hot flashes that feel like chills and fever, depression, being on an "emotional rollercoaster," blackouts, and shaking.

She discussed the impact of menopause on her sexual relationship with her husband and explained how this relationship had changed as she entered menopause and began feeling ill all the time. "We always had a good, happy physical relationship. . . . It was very important as long as it could be. . . . When I was so sick, he never pressured me. One of the worst, crazy things was the decrease in my interest in sex. . . . That was frustrating because it wasn't fair to him. Doctors don't help in that." Brenda hoped that she would eventually emerge from her menopause crisis but seemed not to be very convinced that she would make this transition, and she expressed her feelings of loneliness and helplessness while dealing with these changes. There are times when she is even afraid of going crazy and will try anything to relieve her symptoms. She admitted that it was a time "when mortality really hits you. . . . You lose your will to live."

For other women, we are learning, it is in their fifties that they have their best sex ever. Gail Sheehy suggests that the hormonal changes of menopause may explain, at least in part, why so many women describe a greatly increased store of energy after menopause: "A good deal of the energy of a younger woman goes into producing enough of the hormone progesterone to sustain a possible pregnancy. Postmenopausal women no longer suffer from the handicap of continually fluctuating levels of progesterone."[3] Sheehy also points out that women who experienced mood swings during their menstrual years no longer have to cope with this discomfort after menopause. A great boon of menopause, Sheehy says, is that it forces a woman to tune in to her body's needs and quirks and to stay intimately tuned.

There is still much ambivalence about the subject of menopause, a need to know, yet the fear of knowing. In addition, there is not one menopause, Sheehy notes, but hundreds of variations. Nevertheless, Sheehy's message is a positive one:

> But instead of giving in to frustration over dealing with our uniqueness, we can recognize how lucky we are. In all of human history women's lives were under the coercion of their biology. Today we don't have to be forty-five years old and suddenly estrogen deficient, miserable, and without recourse. We have choices. . . . Despite the trial-and-error state of medical care, a woman at fifty has a second chance. To use it, she must make an alliance with her body and negotiate with her vanity. Today's healthy, active pacesetters will become the pioneers . . . for potent living and wisdom sharing. . . . Yet the reluctance to discuss both the trials and the rewards of moving through the Change of Life has obscured the facts, often keeping younger women in a state of menopausal dread.[4]

It is not surprising that among current menopausal women few learned much about menopause from their mothers. One study found that college-educated women get their facts first from a friend, second from books or the media, and third from their mother—with the last person to advise them being a doctor.[5]

But those times are changing. With the baby boomers now beginning this transition, a growing body of new information and a real interest in talking about the subject is rapidly reshaping our attitudes and perspectives, both male and female.

Fear of Illness

For some of the people we interviewed, health has become a serious preoccupation in their fifties, either because they have contracted a major illness or because a lifelong illness has become more pronounced. One diabetic we interviewed found herself wishing that, as she got older, she did not always have to live in the shadow of this chronic condition. Another woman, Betty, spoke of "the day I woke up after vascular surgery six months ago. I had so many fears about surgery that I was convinced I would not survive it. It was wonderful to wake up and still be alive." For Betty, illness became a life-affirming experience. Afterward, she decided (as did many we interviewed) to be particularly diligent about the important priorities in her life. One common reaction, then, to illness in our fifties is that it can serve as a warning signal that reminds us that procrastination is no longer realistic, and we begin to do those things we really care about. Yet, there were others in our study who came out of life-threatening illnesses bearing a more pessimistic outlook, seeing their illnesses only as a sign of their own mortality. This pessimism, however, was much less frequent in our interviews than optimism about what could still be accomplished.

Michael exemplifies how confrontation with disease and major surgery can affect our basic life structure. During a routine insurance policy examination at the end of his forties, Michael, who had always been healthy and active, was told that his blood pressure was unusually high. He was subsequently advised to undergo a long and complex arterial bypass operation, and he had to put his immediate travel plans and many other matters connected to normal living "on hold."

As he recovered and returned to his previous routine, Michael spent a good deal of time reflecting on his life. "I made the decision to sell the business while I was recovering," Michael noted. "Imagine, I had started it more than twenty years ago, and then suddenly ———. It just no longer seemed very important. It was just too damn stressful. I began growing impatient with other parts of my life as well. One day I decided that was it. I switched careers and took on something with much less responsibility and pressure. And I finally started doing things that really pleased *me* rather than others." Midlife for Michael and those like him who confront their mortality through a life-threatening illness becomes a decade of reckoning.

Several years later, Michael underwent further arterial surgery; however, the impact of this second confrontation with death proved far less physically and psychologically traumatic than the first surgery. By the end of his fifties, Michael had learned how to put things into a healthy, satisfying perspective that met his needs — how to balance the work and nonwork aspects of his life, invest increasing amounts of time in strengthening relationships with his family and friends, take trips to visit old friends, attend family events, and see the country by car, an activity he truly loved.

When Michael was being interviewed, he expressed a growing satisfaction with his life and was clear about what he hoped for in the future. He transmitted a sense of freedom and well-being and was viewed by others as radiating a sense of greater wealth than was the reality. Even though he continues to be aware of his physical vulnerability, he has not become consumed by it. He is moderate in his life-style and eating habits. He balances activity with periods of relaxation and quiet. And, in an unassuming and unglamorous way, his life is full, social, and creative. Michael, indeed, is a free man.

Formal Education, Informal Learning

When asked what they would do differently if they could replay their lives, a number of our interviewees indicated that they would have sought more education earlier in their lives. The women we studied seemed particularly so inclined. Evelyn, for example, had been married at seventeen, then went back to school after she was forty. "There are times," she noted "when I feel like I'd like it the way it was. And there are times I would prefer to have gone to college first."

Another woman, Susan, wished for more education when she was younger for very specific purposes: "I wish I had education on how to deal with children's problems and how to manage our finances well. I needed to know more about myself." Liz, on the other hand, along with a closer relationship with her mother and father (a not uncommon wish), would like "more education . . . to increase my talents." She would like "to read more . . . and to spend less time watching television and going to the movies."

A widespread desire for more education and learning was reflected not only in wishful statements like these but also in individuals' present-day engagement in various learning projects and in preparations for further career challenges.

Our study reveals that many middle-class people in their fifties also love to travel, especially when it means experiencing other cultures.

One fifty-year-old woman, when asked what she would do differently if she had her life to live over again, spoke of spending even more time than she already had in other countries. She is acting on this wish, too, not just regretting it. In the past she spent one year as an exchange teacher in England and hopes, soon, to be able to spend a second year there as well. Veronica spoke of having always wanted to be able "to pick up and leave every couple of years" with her husband. Although her husband has passed away, she still hopes to travel more. She reflected, "Overseas, we were very fortunate because we got to experience many different cultures and make friends that I still keep in touch with today. . . . You learn that there are beautiful people everywhere you go." For many of the world travelers we interviewed, a growing tolerance and wisdom seems to be closely associated with this direct experience of people in other cultures. Gerald talks about "mellowing with age" and attributes this to his experiences in other countries: "Probably the biggest change is that I've graduated from tolerating to a higher stage of accepting. And I think there's a hell of a difference between tolerating and accepting. . . . I think a lot of it has to do with living overseas and seeing through the eyes of other cultures that we are no better than other races or cultures. Especially in Japan. That was an eye-opener. I really refreshed my attitude that just because we are different [that] doesn't make us better."

A renewed interest in reading is also common among the men and women we interviewed. They are often interested in history and other liberal arts disciplines. Formal and informal learning in one's fifties is often learning for its own sake that relates to one's own interests, inner life, or intellectual growth, rather than learning that is meant to be used for instrumental, professional, and employment-related objectives.

This parallels a societal expectation of Eastern cultures that men and women of this age group will turn away from "worldly" interests such as economics, business, politics, science, technology, and athletics and turn toward areas of inner knowledge and philosophical inquiry. They are now expected to move from being doers to being teachers and writers, roles that require more reflection, experience, wisdom, and time in which to think. Indeed, whereas men and women who make major breakthroughs in science and behavioral science have tended to be in their twenties and thirties, revolutions of thought in philosophy and theology are more often made by men and women who are in or near their fifties, or older.

As learners, men and women in their fifties tend to be "experience-rich and theory-poor."[6] They want to make sense of, and find meaning in, their diverse life experiences, rather than simply be exposed to more experiences, as is the case for younger learners. They seek to confirm what they already know and want to acquire an expanded, more elaborate vocabulary to think about, interpret, and discuss what they have already experienced. Hence, they are often hungry for theory — for explanations of their experiences in order to make generalizations and truly understand those experiences. Education becomes a positive tool for generativity and achieving integration in our fifties.

This turning inward, relative to new learning, is poignantly illustrated in the reflections of Eunice, a fifty-two-year-old woman we interviewed. When asked what she would like an imaginary award to say if it could be given to her for her life achievements, Eunice said the award would recognize that "I keep giving and growing despite adversity." Eunice's early life with her family of origin and her first two husbands had been filled with violence and abuse. Like some of the other working-class women we interviewed, she was forced to raise young children on her own with few job skills after her first marriage broke up.

Eunice has spent considerable time reflecting upon these painful experiences and trying to make sense of them. The effort to come to terms with the people who abused her has been painful and difficult, although several years ago, Eunice spent three months with her dying father. That time together helped to heal many of her wounds. She now has a successful relationship, has raised her children, and has recently received her master's degree, specializing in work with abused women. She feels that her ability to overcome her own personal adversities and to keep a sense of optimism has been her biggest asset. The greatest challenge in the decade of her fifties, she says, is how to apply her personal learning to her work with other women who have experienced similar problems.

Many men and women in their fifties begin to find new ways to use their personal life and career experiences to create new careers for themselves. "If I can do this, so can others," they reason. Many new "helping" professionals are born from this phenomenon. And when asked why they chose to learn to do these new things at this stage in their lives, both men and women readily answer, "It was time. I needed to do this before it's too late."

Although adult students frequently refer to completing a previously unfinished degree as the primary motivation for returning to school, their real unfinished agenda is more a need for completion and healing than for the credentials themselves. Our education is a means to integrate and make sense of our life experiences.

Permission to Act

At earlier stages of our adulthood, a need to educate ourselves about the meaning of our experiences might be viewed by others as an admission of failure or as a search for someone to blame. By the time we reach our fifties, we are better able to give ourselves permission to do things that were unthinkable earlier in our lives. As more and more contemporary men and women step out of their previously constrained behaviors in their fifties, others are encouraged to do so, and what were once undiscussable searches for meaning and integrity become more publicly acceptable and can even be viewed as courageous and admirable.

A Transition of Pace

To the external observer, the changes in pace that men and women in their late fifties often undergo may appear to be merely "slowing down." But often something more profound and noteworthy is going on. That slowing down is a manifestation of our changing priorities. We literally shift gears to achieve a pace of activity which is less externally motivated, frantic, and flailing and more self-directed, purposeful, and targeted.

As we fix our attention on the most important things and people in our lives, we begin to "own" our calendars and our time in new ways. We, not others, decide when to take a vacation. We, not others, decide in which project to invest our energies and resources. As we increasingly give ourselves permission to do and be what we ourselves want, we become empowered by being freer to choose. This cycle of focusing, choosing, giving ourselves permission, and ultimately, acting on what we most care about leads to a new sense of generativity.

5

The Mirror of History: Understanding Commonality and Diversity

> History is a prophecy looking backwards.
> —*Anonymous*

Among men and women in their fifties, as we have said, there is a shift from dreams of the future to stories of the past. In the telling of these stories, men and women of this age group often produce what Joseph Campbell would call the "myths" that sustain and even gradually transform a society.[1] While their personal dreams, usually established when they were in their late teens or twenties, have been fulfilled, rejected, or forgotten by the time they are forty or fifty, men's and women's new collective dreams are influential and aid in shaping the personal dreams of the generations that follow. This intergenerational image-making phenomenon explains the mentoring role so often played by men and women in their fifties.

Several of the younger interviewers who participated in our study commented on the debunking of their own personal myths about fifty-year-olds after they had conducted their interviews. "What was most important for me to know," said one of these interviewers, "was that people in their fifties were young, energetic, and normal. One of the men I interviewed felt that each year seemed to get better for him physically, educationally, mentally, and economically."

A new set of myths, or images, is now being constructed by these vital and engaged men and women in their fifties. These images are about a new personal freedom but also often about community. Some fifty-year-old men and women even envision the creation of a utopian world in which people truly and collectively care for one another, for they have often experienced very little true community in their own contemporary lives.[2]

Men's Myths: The Pull Between Freedom and Community

One of our interviewees, Roberto, has been a Catholic priest since 1970. Now, at fifty-two, Roberto is shifting his attention partly away from work and back to family and friends. He says, "As I get older, I realize how my own life commitment to my work has sometimes interfered with my relationships, in particular with my parents. I want to allow more time to spend with my family and friends, as well as time for myself. On occasion I have felt the effects of overextending for others, and I am attempting to become more comfortable with allowing time away from work to enjoy this time in my life."

For someone who has devoted his entire life to a cause or a career, as Roberto has, this new orientation to relationships is often stressful. Roberto is simultaneously looking for a closer community with his own family and friends and for more autonomy in order to spend time alone. Paradoxically, Roberto and many other men of his age are inclined to hear two kinds of inner voices: one that speaks to their need for community and another that speaks to their need for individuality and separation from the community.

This conflict is addressed by a new myth about men in their fifties that has come to be known as the "Wild Man" myth, and has been popularized by Robert Bly.[3] Most cultures, Bly points out in his provocative exploration of masculinity, have an abundance of stories about a Wild Man who defies or avoids contact with the civilized world and comes to be admired at a distance by those who remain in the village or city. At some point, he is captured or tempted by "some beautiful woman" into returning to society. Once back in the civilized world, he is domesticated, ultimately loses his "ferociousness" of spirit, and dies as a lonely and broken shell of the vital man he once was.

In their fifties, many men no longer find any real justification for continuing with socially acceptable "domesticity"— whether as businessmen, professionals, or bricklayers. Their Wild Man voice demands to be heard again. It is a voice that seems to be particularly persuasive after or during some significant life failure, perhaps the loss of a job or a traumatic divorce. However, it also can appear after a man achieves some form of personal security or independence—the final payment on his house, or the settlement of some other long-standing debt.

A common scenario is as follows: the reemerged Wild Man changes or leaves his job. He unhooks from wife and family. He moves away from the city into the country. He takes up art or woodcarving, teaching or landscaping, skiing, volleyball, or perhaps long-distance running. He becomes an entrepreneur. He starts a small restaurant, sells real estate, remodels houses, or establishes a small publishing company for obscure poets. The details may differ, but the pattern is remarkably similar.

Keith, for instance, has been labeled "the bright and compassionate Mad Hatter" by one of his students in the psychology class he teaches at a community college. It is a title he thoroughly enjoys. Having abandoned a traditional and secure career as an academic psychologist, Keith now works at a much lower salary for a public service agency assisting families in crisis and teaches only part-time in order to give him more time for his family and for recreation. It represented a start, he confided, of "selective disengagement from current commitments."

Usually, the move to a new career leaves a fifty-year-old Wild Man with greater freedom and potential capacity to have an impact because he typically moves to a much smaller organization. In addition, the "breaking away" provides a psychological moratorium, a pause, that can be used to explore alternative identities and a new sense of self. Jim, the man we described in Chapter Two, who gave up his wife and family in order to move to California and write, also exemplifies the psychological moratorium gained by listening to one's Wild Man. But Jim's life also exemplifies the heavy personal costs often associated with this moratorium.

Loss, grieving, and depression typically accompany the emergence of the Wild Man, as long-term commitments are abandoned and outgrown. Once he can come to accept the loss, the old self is discarded. Thus, for the modern Wild Man, the choice is often between a "broken heart" caused by the abandonment of that which is known and cherished, and an "abandoned heart" caused by the failure to acknowledge and act upon one's true, yet-to-be discovered personal destiny.

Like the biblical figure of Jonah, we cannot run away forever from voices from other rooms that beckon us to try on a new personal identity. Eventually, as happened to Jonah, something will capture us, carry us to our destiny, and cast us out upon new ground. Our twentieth-century Wild Man will be required to construct a new reality and a new sense of life's purpose if he chooses this relatively radical route to freedom in his fifties.

There is another pattern that men in their fifties frequently encounter. Although they may want to be freed from the kind of responsibility that domesticity represents, it is not uncommon for them to find that, eventually, they want a more meaningful kind of community.

Most men, from very early in their lives, tend to seek autonomy and define themselves in terms of how they differ from other people. During the early years of their development, their closest relationships most often are with their mothers, their teachers, and others who are decidedly different from them because of gender.

By the time they reach midlife, however, men find themselves increasingly concerned about connectedness rather than differentiation. Having spent all of their adult lives trying to "make it to the top" as individuals and become less dependent on people such as parents, bosses, and wives, they now discover that they feel isolated from others.

As they move into their fifties, men often try to establish a community or a "life-style enclave" with the people who live and work around them or with whom they share common interests. They want to feel as if they belong and begin paying attention to their voices from other rooms that speak about increased sociability, a renewed commitment to neighbors and the local community, or the importance of intimacy and interpersonal commitment.

Women's Myths: Independence

And what of women in their fifties? Which myths are at play in their lives? Do they too strive to escape from their early lives of domesticity and careers as well?

One prevalent old myth that shaped today's fifty-year-old middle-class women has been called "the Cinderella Syndrome."[4] Most women who grew up in the United States in the post–World War II years of the 1940s and 1950s thought that their Prince Charming would come along one day and care for them for the rest of their lives. All the woman had to do was be pretty enough and nice enough to attract Prince Charming. This particular myth has been responsible for many of the disillusionments among women that were revealed by the women's movement of the 1960s and 1970s. As it became increasingly clear that there were few Prince Charmings in the world and that being Cinderella was not as continuously fulfilling as it might have seemed, women came to understand that their futures were their own to make.

In addition, contemporary middle-class women who are now in their fifties grew up in an era when most women were expected to devote their greatest attention to the family and home, even if they were working full-time outside the home. This orientation toward others was developed early in their lives under a caregiver — usually their mother — who was very much like them. They did not experience the difference from their caregivers and teachers that men did. For women, affiliation with other people seems commonplace. As a result, women are often willing to become more dependent on, or at least interdependent with, other people in an effort to remain closely affiliated with them. This willingness to sacrifice their own identities and independence in order to retain the affection and support of other people changes by the time they have reached their forties and fifties. Many are tired of being the source of all sacrifice and accommodation and wish to make a strong statement to the world—particularly to those who are closest to them—about their desire for greater autonomy.

Our interviews reveal that women do create and act out dreams and myths about freedom and autonomy, especially if these dimensions have been absent in their earlier lives.[5] In some cases, women's new identities have characteristics similar to those of Bly's Wild Man. Donna, for example, made a decision to abandon her marriage and her position as director of a broadcasting company and to start a new life. Her new image of what was possible took shape when she decided to take some time off and go to a local spa. She recalls, "I went to the spa on vacation but discovered it was not a very pleasant place at all. In fact, it was terrible. The special part of it all was that I realized that I did not have to stay. I left, hopped a plane to Maui, and had a wonderful week by myself. I broke out of the mold of having to do what I said I would do. It was great."

That trip and the sudden realization of what she had done were transformative for Donna. She became a fiercely independent woman who refused to conform any longer to other people's expectations. She decided to resign from her job in order to concentrate on ending her marriage. However, unlike many of the men we interviewed, Donna eventually returned to her previous job to continue her career. Of her two greatest successes, as she reviewed and evaluated her life, remaining in a responsible position while "not giving up" her newfound autonomy was one of them.

While there are many women such as Donna who abandon long-term marriages, perhaps to start their own small businesses or to return to school to obtain a professional degree,[6] for most women, their fifties decade is an opportunity for greater clarification of that true self that they have always possessed but could never allow to flourish.

Rena, a fifty-year-old woman in real estate whom we interviewed, laughed delightedly when asked to describe what she

would like to have said by someone giving her an award to honor
her achievements. She stated with enthusiasm, "I'm me!" If she
ever received such an award, she added, she would want it to
acknowledge that she now has more control of her life while at
the same time can choose to abandon some of this control when
she wants to explore an unpredictable future.

Debra wanted us to know that if she could live her life
over again, she would have "listened to my own head instead
of someone else's." In recent months, she has begun to listen
to her long-muted internal voices and is questioning her work
as a real-estate agent. While Debra doesn't know yet exactly
what it is she would like to do, she is determined to start over
again in a new and different field.

For some women, however, dreams of autonomy are accompanied by fears about being alone. Jill, for instance, who
has been married three times and describes herself as a coward
who wants autonomy and independence, openly admits, "I am
scared of being alone, being on my own, being over fifty. Plus,
you know what the big thing is with me? I've been divorced twice
before. How do I explain that to my family?" Jill doesn't think
she can remain married to her current husband and has been
evaluating the financial consequences of a divorce. What she most
dreads is not the new exploration that a period of being alone
might bring, but having "some little apartment with the bed coming off the wall" in a whole life of loneliness and alienation.

Another interviewee, Doris, is also ambivalent about autonomy. When asked how she would like her life to have been
different, she is deeply reflective.

> Looking back on it, both my husband and I were
> pretty good students, and we were married very
> young — but I probably would have gotten more
> education. Thinking back on it now . . . I was one
> of the first ones in our group of friends to get even
> a part-time job. I had male friends that said, "You're
> one of those women libbers." You know, it was a
> big thing because I went to work for two or three
> hours a day. . . . At one point — even today — if my

husband had died when my children were young, it would have been hard to support them. I now admire women who are able to make it on their own. They don't have to have a husband to support them. . . . Had I had just a little more life, I still would never regret being married young and having a child young, and that sort of thing. Maybe you can't have both.

For both men and women, new images have to be tested against the financial and emotional costs of abandoning older images to discover what degree of change is truly best for each individual.

Many women's lives, especially, now reflect a number of activities: school, marriage, children, career, jobs, family, and volunteerism. No longer is there any one right way to juggle, integrate, and sequence these various aspects of life, which increases the need for each person to consciously set priorities. The new images that will come from these men's and women's lives will convey a collective set of possibilities, rather than one new right way to live. But they will be passed on in old ways.

Throughout history, women's ways of knowing and learning have been informal and interpersonal.[7] Women have passed along their "stories," in which knowledge, skills, and wisdom reside, from one to the other and from generation to generation in settings outside formal schools — at the water well, over baskets of laundry, in the marketplace, over the back fence, during neighborhood and family coffee klatches, and in whatever other setting has been available to them in a given culture at a given time.

Today, once they have defined a common interest or need, women frequently form an organization in order to share their knowledge and frustrations and to seek strategies for taking collective action.[8]

There are millions of such groups in the United States. Their potential to shape the personal lives, career lives, community lives, and workplaces of the future has just begun to become apparent, and part of the knowledge they will be passing on will be the collective possibilities for setting priorities and learning one's true values that have been discovered by the women who are in their fifties now and who came to their knowledge by living through three turbulent decades.

Our Historical Context

How do the personal and collective dreams of our fifties relate to the historical context in which we grew up? Those of us now in our fifties have lived through an exceptionally rich and diverse period of historical, social, and cultural change, not only here in the United States but throughout the world. What sense are we to make of this change? How has it molded and transformed us? Are we simply products of our era or do universal threads of historical commonality weave us together into some uniform understanding of what our fifties are all about?

Common Values

We in the current generation of fifty- to sixty-year-old men and women were born in the years between 1932 and 1941, just after the Crash of '29 and just before "the good War" — World War II — engulfed our world. In many respects, our early childhood years were spent during a period of U.S. history when the "old" values still prevailed, when the work ethic was alive and well, and when a certain link of national "glue" bound people together for common purposes, purposes that everyone seemingly understood. Middle-class Americans, the group we are focusing on in this book, certainly experienced these common threads.

During the 1930s, being in one's fifties was viewed by most people as simply being old. Grandma, in her fifties, wore corsets and house dresses, while Grandpa looked forward to retirement, if he was lucky enough to still have a job in those harsh economic times. Our parents were often newlyweds, struggling to come out of the Depression, beginning families, working hard to move into, or stay in, the middle class, and seeking to protect us children as much as they could from the hard times they had known. Even if there was little money, there was an esprit de corps that held families together and a deep faith that things would get better. Everyone was in the same boat, and it was believed that the best ship's captains would survive and prosper. As children, we were told that "anything was possible" and that, with a little effort, we could "reach for the stars."

Hollywood, Baseball, and FDR

In the 1930s, one thing that everyone in the United States shared was the image of desirable upper-class life that was created in Hollywood. Hollywood movies were also filled with romance, big stars, and happy endings. Stars like Clark Gable, Bing Crosby, Alice Faye, and Betty Grable sent us autographed glossy photographs, and we collected these images of success and glamour with a real passion just as we did the tradable baseball cards packaged with bubble gum. Joe DiMaggio and the New York Yankees personified major league baseball, while the "Bums," the Brooklyn Dodgers, were our sentimental favorites. Leo Durocher, Pee Wee Reese, and Gil Hodges were household names for both boys and girls. Jackie Robinson, the first black major league baseball player, would soon emerge as a symbol of courage and a role model in the ongoing search for racial equality. Hollywood and baseball provided a common vocabulary and a shared set of experiences all across America.

On the political front, Franklin D. Roosevelt represented something of a "Great Father" in homes of Democrats but was seen as a "Great Devil" in homes of Republicans and many destitute Americans. He so dominated our childhood memories of the government of the United States of America that many of us thought he might end up being our president forever. For many of us, he was America, and America meant hope. His wife, Eleanor, was a tower of strength, publicly active, caring, and socially conscious. Without calling herself a feminist, Mrs. Roosevelt provided us with a female role model that remained indelibly etched in our minds as a contrast to our own more domestic and homebound mothers. This couple, aristocratic and at the same time egalitarian, were like parents to America, rebuilding trust and belief in our future for many of us at a time when an entire new economic structure was being formed and a global war, already raging in Europe and Asia, would soon involve our nation across oceans to the east and to the west.

Technicolor Dreams, Radio, and Broadway

For those of us who dared to dream in the 1930s, our dreams were nurtured and technicolored by the blossoming U.S. entertainment industry. Films, radio, big bands, and musical comedy theater filled our eyes and ears with romance, ideal love, and patriotism.

"Jack Armstrong, the All American Boy," "The Shadow," "Let's Pretend," "George Burns and Gracie Allen," "Fibber McGee and Molly" — the message of many radio programs was that with hard work, a sense of right, and a little luck, all would be well. They created an image of hope. You only had to believe. Or so we thought.

The Wizard of Oz, Shirley Temple as *Rebecca of Sunnybrook Farm, Gone with the Wind,* Fred Astaire and Ginger Rogers, Judy Garland and Mickey Rooney — movies taught us to dream, and the messages were that women were glamorous, men were handsome, men and women fall in love, and in spite of problems and challenges, they live happily ever after. The image created by Hollywood was also one of hope. You only had to believe. Or so we thought.

Cole Porter, Ethel Merman, Bob Hope, Fannie Brice, *The Ziegfeld Follies, Anything Goes* — Broadway musical comedies and the 78-rpm records that brought them to us taught us that everything works out okay in the end. They brought light-heartedness and a distraction from those Depression years into the lives of our worried parents and inspired us to sing and dance in the privacy of our own bedrooms or on the polished linoleum of our kitchen floors and to reach for our own imagined stardom, in whatever ways we chose. Set in interesting places and times, boy met girl, trouble began, boy won out over trouble, and boy and girl lived happily ever after. The image created by musical comedy was one of hope. You only had to believe. Or so we thought.

In this idealized, emerging middle-class world, dinner ta-
bles were surrounded by family members each night. Dinner
time was quiz time, vocabulary game time — a time to prove
to our parents that we were good students. Stories from each
family member's day were part of our dinner-table habits.

Sundays were visiting days for us back then — grandparents, cousins, neighbors, our parents' best friends. It seemed
a little boring at times, but when we did go visiting, we were
always dressed in our Sunday best.

Summer evenings were for stoop ball, hopscotch, and stick
ball. And when there weren't too many cars passing by for those
of us who lived in suburbia or the city, hide-and-seek, ring ale-
vio, kick-the-can, jumping rope, and catching fireflies in a jar
occupied our attention and our energies. We were a part of a
group. We were part of a neighborhood. We belonged.

Elementary school for many of us living in the cities or
the suburbs was called grammar school or public school then.
Our teachers were fearsome. We sat in alphabetical order. The
principal was always in command. We got paste-on stars and
acknowledgment for good grades. We learned early that achievement and "reaching for the stars" was what it was all about.

"The Good War"

World War II came crashing into our lives on Sunday, Decem-
ber 7, 1941, over the radio, when Japan bombed Pearl Har-
bor. Life changed in many ways, yet our young lives remained
fundamentally the same. For many of us, there was wartime
rationing of meat, sugar, gasoline, and tires. None of us minded,
then. For those of us in the middle class, we felt lucky and always seemed to have enough. Our dependable parents saw to
that.

We learned to save tin cans, to peel the tinfoil off chew-
ing gum wrappers, to knit squares of wool or socks for our
brothers going overseas, and to buy war bonds for $18.75.

We were proudly patriotic. We sang "Praise the Lord and
Pass the Ammunition," gave patriotic speeches at school assem-
blies, and got teary-eyed at parades.

Mrs. Miniver and General Douglas MacArthur were our kind of heroine and hero. We knew what was right and good and what we had to do. When we finally did win the war, our trust and faith in the United States of America was reaffirmed. By then, in 1945, some of us who are now in our fifties were just entering kindergarten; others were on our way into high school. Those few years of difference in our ages made a big difference in our images and our experiences. The energy in the country was high, as life returned to "normal." A peacetime economy moved into high gear, and middle-class Americans began to build the most productive and envied society our world had ever known.

Clear Roles

Our job as middle-class children and young teen-agers was, first, to be the best students we could be in our classes and, later, to see that we got into the best colleges to which we could be accepted. Our father's job was to support the family. Mother's job was to see that we had good food, clean clothes, and a neat house. In those days, everyone knew his or her role and sought to be as good at it as he or she could be. The United States was still glued together by the euphoria of victory and our determination to make our earlier dreams come true.

For many of us, our high school cheerleaders and football heroes were our stars. Our role models were clear and real. We had learned to be resourceful during the war. Now, we applied our creative abilities to book reports, school plays, and piano lessons. Whatever our actual status was, we knew what it was supposed to become. Rules were clear. Being delinquent was usually, by today's standards, relatively harmless. At the worst, it meant we had been caught drinking beer or seen necking in a car. As middle-class kids, we were shielded from drugs and violence.

Ethnicity

Ethnicity defined our middle-class neighborhoods, and crossing neighborhood lines often brought confrontation and conflict.

Racial and cultural diversity was not seen as a positive community characteristic. If a family that was different from the majority moved to our block, it often caused a neighborhood crisis. If a few of us struck up a friendship with someone outside our own ethnic group, we felt a bit noble, at least inside.

For some of us, family arguments about who should be our friends were one of our first real losses of innocence. Even after we had fought and won "a good war," in which millions had been killed because they did not belong to the right group, we heard prejudiced statements and narrow-minded opinions coming from our own parents' mouths. This lack of tolerance began to bother some of us. Perhaps our parents were not the fount of all virtue and wisdom after all. As we edged further toward our own identities in adolescence, we began to question those whose authority had previously defined our values and beliefs.

The Changing Political Landscape

By the time we went off either to college, to marry, or to find a job — in some cases, all three — a popular war hero, General Dwight D. Eisenhower, had become our Republican president. The new middle-class prosperity pushed many socially conscious Democrats to vote with the Republicans. The atomic bomb, which we believed had both shortened the conflict and won the war for us, reframed our lives, as did the emerging Cold War with the Soviet Union and its allies. The birth of television glued us to a tiny screen to watch wrestling matches, Milton Berle, and the "Ed Sullivan Show." Although we were still being seen as those generous Americans who had taken on the gargantuan task of rebuilding war-torn Europe, a change in our attitude about our seemingly endless responsibility for others began to reveal itself.

"How to spot a Communist in our business" was a major theme in a booklet about the Communist Party in the United States. Soviet spy rings became front page news. Suspicion and fear turned our daily attention to the McCarthy hearings on television. Howdy Doody occupied the kids, but we, as young adults, were tuned in to loyalty panels and the fear of "Commies." Soon, we were no longer sure who the good guys and the bad guys really were. The Russians, our former friends, were now our enemies. The Germans, our former enemies, were becoming our new friends. Loyalties shifted. Patriotism was questioned. Our neatly glued-together America was slowly coming apart.

The Ungluing of America—The 1950s and 1960s

It was during the 1950s and early 1960s that we, then in our late twenties, thirties, and early forties, began, as a group, to look inside ourselves. Our nation's wars in Korea and Vietnam were not supported by everyone as World War II had been. Just why were we fighting "over there" in Asia anyway? The draft was still part of our lives, and many of the men among us found themselves being sent to rugged and alien battlefields but without reasons we could all believe in.

Although we were still a relatively obedient and patriotic group, a few of us began to question our country's role in the world. We realized that our parents no longer had the answers we now sought—nor did the news commentators, the movies, our friends, nor our teachers. There seemed no longer to be one voice, but many voices.

As we began the second half of the twentieth century in the United States, our coherent, once understandable country had begun its long divided period. What we did not know, as we settled into new sprawling Levittowns of sameness with our new shiny appliances and new babies, was that we would never again know a country that was not seriously divided into many splintered pieces. Our sense of national purpose began to fade, and we turned inward to nurture our own personal well-being as an alternative to seeking meaning in our external, national life. An era of diversity had begun. We who grew up in a time when sameness was encouraged had few tools with which to work and few mentors to emulate. Our old values were being questioned, while few new values were available for adoption.

New Reforms Breed New Images

The civil rights movement of the 1960s spotlighted the dispari-
ties that existed between our old values and our emerging new
values.

For some of us, the efforts of black Americans to gain full
equality struck familiar chords with the language of patriotism
that we had learned in our World War II childhoods. We had
been fighting then for equality. Images of the horrors of the
Holocaust and other instances of inhuman cruelty played deeply
within us. How could we now refuse equal opportunity to a
growing segment of our own citizens? We knew it was a person's
character, not skin color or ethnic group, that was the important ingredient that made success available to every American.
Wasn't this the lesson taught to us by our immigrant grandparents and our Depression-era parents?

For others, however, the civil rights movement threat-
ened a further erosion of the old values and life-styles that they
had been taught. Separation, not integration, was the American way, they thought. Sameness and homogeneity, not diversity and difference, were necessary if the America they knew
was to survive. The battle for the second half of the twentieth-
century had been joined.

As we made choices about race, religion, and life-style,
some of us opted for the old values that were familiar and comfortable; others of us began the search for some useful definitions of what were to become our new values.

Middle-class women, in particular, were making life-style
choices and developing new images, venturing out of the house
into the community and the workplace. Mothers working outside the home were relatively rare then, especially in suburbia,
and were viewed as somewhat self-indulgent, in spite of the fact
that millions of women in the lower and upper classes and on
farms had always carried on work or volunteer activities outside the home and continued to do so. The mainstream expectations for middle-class men centered around their roles as breadwinners and community leaders. Few questioned that these
functions represented an American ideal.

However, the public's division over the civil rights movement was beginning to infiltrate kitchens, parlors, and family rooms across the nation while the women's movement — sparked by Betty Friedan's book *The Feminine Mystique*[9] — began to make male and female role definitions much more complex. The quest for equality among the races spread rapidly into a quest for equality between the sexes. The typical middle-class American family, of which many of us had once been an integral part, was never to be the same again.

The Vietnam War only exacerbated the divisions that were tearing apart the American quilt, feeding the ongoing controversy about what was "right" and what was "wrong" with our country. Diversity of opinion erupted into open conflict on college campuses. The peace movement resulted in entire groups of young adults moving into alternative life-styles in a clear rejection of their parents' values. New poets such as Allen Ginsberg, the philosophies of the East as espoused by gurus such as Alan Watts, and even political revolutionaries such as Fidel Castro and Mao Tse-tung became alternative images for various groups of American youth to emulate. Many young people now believed that the American Dream had failed to provide equally and fairly for everyone. They began to search for new images that would better match their ideals.

Beyond Images, Toward New Roles

Those of us now in our fifties, who were then mostly in our thirties, were bewildered and angered. Some of us identified and joined forces with our younger defiant baby-boomer brothers and sisters, forsaking suburbia to participate in experiments with communes or collaborative living arrangements. Others of us chose to drop out of the "rat race" we had been led into — or had walked freely into — in our earlier years. Still others, believing in the ultimate reconciliation of old with new values, set out to reform the nation's mainstream institutions and organizations or to create new, alternative businesses that were more collaborative and humanistic.

As we moved out of the Vietnam period, exhausted and more divided as a nation than ever before, the late 1970s and

1980s found many of us in the middle of our own midlife crises, questioning our life-styles more intensely than we had earlier. Our children, heading toward adulthood, seemed bereft of role models on which to base their own lives.

Many of our daughters were angry with their mothers who, by and large, had remained careerless and had failed to provide them with adequate lessons to guide them into satisfying futures. Paradoxically, many mothers were themselves looking to their often more independent daughters for guidance about how to reenter the work force or return to school.

Our sons had begun viewing their fathers' lives of self-sacrifice for family as futile guides for their own decisions about their futures in a rapidly changing world. As these young men, and many young women too, became more skilled in the new emerging information-age technologies, it was their fathers, and mothers, who now began to feel left behind. Parents began to turn to their children for technical information, guidance, and advice. The generation gap had effectively been turned on its head.

Between the 1960s and the 1980s, divorce became commonplace enough for virtually everyone to question whether the model of one monogamous lifetime marriage was an ideal that was now passé. Life-lengthening medical technology raised serious moral dilemmas, as well as economic ones, about responsibilities to oneself and to others. Single and surrogate parenthood, abortion, artificial insemination, DNA discoveries—these new life choices and technical advances all seemed to conspire to defeat the models of family, work, and community, and one right way for everyone with which those of us in our fifties had grown up.

Reinventing Roles in Our Fifties

An extraordinary shift in consciousness has occurred over the past few decades and it continues today. Our world has dramatically changed from a relatively certain one, where each person knew his or her clearly defined role, to one that is exceedingly complex and uncertain, where everyone seems to be preoccupied with self-redefinition. New models of behavior are being called for in every arena of life. Our formal educations, no matter how extensive or prestigious, seem obsolete and of limited value now that lifelong learning has become necessary to keep up with the rapid changes caused largely by new technology.

Our work roles are being redefined. In some cases, our anxieties about finding and keeping jobs are heightened as we feel increasingly unprepared to do the jobs that will have to be done in the future. Our organizations are questioning the very foundations of their existence and examining their missions and purposes, while raising questions about the nature of the leadership that will prove to be effective in the future. Effective leaders now stand in the middle of their intersecting "network organizations," orchestrating many parts while ever newer generations of computers provide wider access to information that, only a short time ago, was accessible only to a few. Hierarchical organization charts are out of fashion. Flattened, streamlined organizations are in. Linear is out. Cyclical is in. Triangles are out. Networks, fishnets, and spider-webs are in. Single-minded CEOs are out. Teams are in. Dress codes are out. A more casual world of attire is in.

The personal self-indulgences of 1980s yuppies are giving way to yearnings for simpler life-styles, as young baby-boom adults turn their attention to raising families of their own — juggling, balancing, and integrating their multiple roles of parent, worker, learner, and community member.

For those of us in our fifties, living through this tumultuous period has irrevocably altered our lives. Until recently, some of us thought it would be a relatively simple process to find our own answers. We would simply go on turning the pages of the same book from which our parents learned. Others of us realized early on that it was not going to be. We would have to learn from a different book.

Now, in our fifties, we all must sort ourselves out once again. We try to understand our ambivalence, our hesitations, and the complex forces that move us forward into reinvention. It is not an easy task.

Our history does matter. The tension between the old images of our childhoods and youth and our new circumstances and understanding is what drives the development of our new roles and new behaviors in mid life. Just as we in our fifties are creating new myths today, those in their forties who follow us will find that their own myth-making processes owe a debt to the historical times through which they have lived.

In this way, each succeeding generation must ultimately find its own vitality and fulfillment, as each individual man and woman struggles for generativity within his or her own time and place in history.

6

Friends and Lovers:
The Quest for Relationship
and Autonomy

You are never too old to take steps toward freedom.
—Anonymous

Our fifties have often been described as golden years, a time for savoring our accomplishments and living off our accumulated goodwill in terms of parenting, colleagueship, and friendship. Yet for many men and women in their fifties, the gold is tarnished. They feel isolated from their children. They have little time or energy to keep up long-term friendships. The people they care most about either move away or die. Geographical distance quickly becomes a solid wall of separation and silence. To make new friends oftentimes seems too difficult.

But we can, if we wish, make many gains as well. Even though we typically lose our children in terms of active, everyday parenting, in their place we often acquire grandchildren. And we are able to form new and sometimes more fulfilling adult-to-adult relationships with our children now that they have experienced independence.

Once into our fifties, many of us move toward a more inner-directed life. As a result, we tend to abandon some of our old friendships. We cultivate fewer but closer friends as we grow older. Thus, while some friends are lost, this decision is often made of our own choosing.

Connectedness and Freedom

As illustrated in Chapter Five, men and women in the United States often experience a conflict between their fierce individualism and their simultaneous need for community and commitment. Alexis de Toqueville observed this tension in the nineteenth century,[1] and it is no less true today.[2] We don't really know if we want to be left alone, with our individual rights being paramount, or if we want to be part of a community, with a strong commitment to collective responsibility.

Role Models

June, a fifty-two-year-old divorcée, spoke of her fear of becoming too dependent on other people. She worries about nursing homes, poverty, and cancer — about almost anything that would require her, as one of Tennessee Williams's characters says, to "depend on the kindness of strangers." In order to minimize the chances of losing her autonomy, June returned to college to obtain a degree in order to be more qualified in the job market and, therefore, more economically independent. Many of the women we interviewed have followed a similar course. For June, it was her father who gave her the will to be independent; it was he who showed her the way to obtain this independence.

In the first half of life, the women in our study had typically looked toward their mothers — and other women — as their role models. May, a fifty-six-year-old real-estate broker still adores her mother and a special teacher. Her mother is "a queen of a woman, and very, very bright. I was an only child. My father died just a few weeks ago. I didn't get along with him. I came from a family that believed women should be kept barefoot and pregnant and [keep] their mouths shut! . . . The person who had the greatest impact on me was a teacher — a nun — in Catholic school during a time I was really rebellious. It was this nun who was able to help me with the ability to be both autonomous and caring for others. I'll never forget that woman." May was able to learn both affiliation and autonomy from other women. But many women look toward their fathers as role models in the second half of their lives. It was their fathers, for these women, who ultimately taught them about autonomy and ambition; it was their mothers who taught them about accommodation and affiliation.

Fifty-year-old men, by contrast, often spoke of an emerging desire to connect with other people and of their desire to emulate more closely their mothers' or wives' commitment to the welfare of others. The newfound interest in relationships, however, often comes too late. Just at the point when a fifty-year-old man wants to establish a closer relationship with his wife, she often has begun looking for greater autonomy and interests outside the home and marriage. Just at the point when many men wish to establish more active and supportive relationships with their children, their offspring graduate from high school or college and are off and running in pursuit of their own careers and the establishment of their own families.

Paul, who was fired during the recession from his management position at age fifty-six, feels socially isolated. His relationship with his wife has changed for the better—they are much more equal than in the past—but he has only a limited social network. "Most of my energies are directed toward my relationship with my wife," he says. "I don't have a lot of room in my life for close friends, although I regret I don't devote more time to developing and maintaining friendships. Most of my friendships gradually grew more distant and less intimate the older I got. . . . My relationships with the kids are not as close as I'd like them. I see them more as friendships now than parent-child relationships. My eighty-five-year-old mother needs a lot of caring for and consumes a lot of my energies now."

The Value of Friendship

For most men entering their fifties, forming new friendships or enriching old ones is often difficult. They are used to forming relationships primarily in connection with their jobs while their wives took primary responsibility for forming and maintaining non–work-related friendships. In their fifties, men want to form close friendships with other men and with women other than their wives, friendships that relate to their newfound voices and priorities. However, the demands of work, family, and self still leave little time for friendships, unless men focus on this area as a priority.

Some of our needs for deeper and richer friendships can be satisfied by our mates or significant others. Bryan and his wife, for example, have been married for thirty years. With their seven children now out of the house, he and his wife have "the freedom" at last to become real friends again. Bryan talked with a great deal of excitement about their "emancipation" and the enjoyment he and his wife now have doing things together without the children, including a trip to visit a number of people they had been friends with before family life and geographical distance made it necessary for him to focus on his career and his wife on the upbringing of their children. The development of those old friendships into new deeper relationships may not be essential, or even pragmatically possible, yet Bryan and his wife may have satisfied a need to reconnect with those who once gave their lives special meaning.

Of course, there are others such as Val. Friends are more important to her now than ever: "I love them all," she reflected. "They are my own; they're attached to me; they're mine!" Usually, however, we find that there simply is not enough time to sustain all of the rich and important relationships from our forties and earlier years.

Roberto, for instance, observes that his role as a priest requires frequent moves from one area of the country to another. Long distance relationships in our "temporary society"[3] often cannot be sustained. However, Roberto has discovered how to compensate for distance: "It has made me appreciate my separated friends all the more. . . . I have come to the point in my life when I grasp the moment when I am with my friends, making the best of the time I have with them."

But many, like Noreen, have not been able to sustain what once were close relationships after such old friends have moved away. Noreen says, "There are four of us [women] who have been friends for a long time, and we see less of each other because we don't live near each other. Their children are older and they are freer now. Two of them have gone back to work, so they are not free any more. But we see them in the summer for two weeks. There has been a little bit of a change because now we look back over so many years. We look at each other and we say, 'Can you believe this?' and they look at me and say, 'Oh gosh! How many years have you got to go now?' So it's kind of a good change in a way, I think. Just the time passing."

Several of the fifty-year-olds we interviewed spoke of renewed or more extensive relationships that came about as a result of the recent loss of another important relationship in their lives, whether through divorce, death, or a child's growing up and moving away. When asked about the important people in her life, Lotte said:

> My friends have taken the place of my fam-
> ily. . . . My family lives far away, and I have not
> been able to communicate with them. I am close
> to my brother but sometimes don't talk to him for
> months. I currently have wonderful relationships
> with my friends. We have fun together, act as a
> support system and never fight — very rarely. I think
> I can be straight with them, or if something comes
> up, I take a real good look at them and I might
> not be friends with them. I had one close friend that
> I used to do a lot of things together with. Then it
> changed because the interest wasn't there. I think
> people's energy level changes. The need that I must
> have had to see [her], for example, is not there any-
> more. It kind of changes. And the people that I have
> had discord with are no longer friends.

Nevertheless, there is a void in Lotte's life that does not get read-ily filled by friends: "All relationships will have problems. The closer you are, the more problems you will have. I found my-self feeling tense before I called [a certain person]. If a relation-ship is not nurturing, I don't want to have it."

Our findings were similar for many people we studied who were trying, in the middle of their lives, to substitute casual friends for other significant and more intimate relationships. While this substitution may work at other times, it appears that the decade of their fifties, for most, is a time when the need for a few significant relationships becomes critical. Solid friendships deepen over the years. By the time we reach our fifties, we treasure those friendships that have lasted a long time. They are truly irreplaceable. Once we reach our fifties, there just isn't enough time left in life to establish the kinds of friendships that stretch across a lifetime.

Without close relationships to nurture new growth and development, fifty-year-old men and women often appear to feel alienated from others and fall into a state of stagnation. Even the worlds of work and community service are rarely substitutes at this juncture in life for the intimate relationships that only husbands, wives, lovers, or close friends can provide. These one-to-one intimates help to give us the inner strength and comfort that we desperately need in our fifties if we are to be growth-oriented and generative.

Therefore, a primary task for individuals in their fifties is to find a level of comfort in relationships and nurturing as they go through the process of reinventing themselves. This is new territory for many men and may, at first, seem strange and frightening. But allowing interdependence to grow and develop can be one of the most generative and freeing things a man in his fifties can do.

Many women, on the other hand, find new generativity in their fifties through an increased sense of autonomy and independence. But they too need to maintain the close relationships, the special friendships.

Our fifties is our time to reintegrate the people who matter the most to us back into our lives, before it is too late.

A New Kind of Intimacy

The relationship that is most likely to be sustained in this period of reinventing ourselves is perhaps, surprisingly, with our spouse or significant other. While our children have often left home by the time we reach fifty and our friendships have changed and become fewer, our partner is often still there to support us and be our companion. This central, intimate relationship can be a major source of generativity.

In spite of the rates of breakup and divorce and in spite of the differences in the rhythms and energy levels between men and women in this decade, care and friendship, born of many years of living together, often transcend the conflicts we have been discussing.

Care and friendship can be especially important when one of the partners suffers from poor health, and the nature of the relationship must shift. Madeline, one of our interviewees, finds that although her sex life with her husband is now diminished due to his medical problems, "We still do a lot of cuddling and kissing and talking. The children are grown, and we are spending more time than ever by ourselves. This is good for our relationship. Except for the sex, it has never been better."

A health crisis may also precipitate a woman's acceptance of autonomy and a man's acceptance of community. Harriet's husband to whom she has been married for more than thirty-five years, underwent two major surgeries while she was in her fifties. She reminisced:

> As one waits outside the operating room, thoughts return of him waiting while you gave birth to your children. Now, the marital shoe is on the other foot. Days in the intensive care unit are long, as blood pressure and other vital signs are monitored. As he nods in and out of consciousness, the thought of losing him, forever, becomes real and, at times, overwhelming and frightening. Your own children "stand by" and offer support. Now, the parental shoe is on the other foot, as child and parent reverse roles. When he recuperates and is well again, the rhythm of our lives has changed. He is the more cautious one; you are the risk taker. He has confronted death; you have confronted aloneness.

Beatrice, a fifty-year-old owner and operator of a day care center, pointed out that all she and her husband, Dwain, had done for the last fourteen years was simply raise children, to the neglect of their own intimacy, and that she only now has begun to feel close to him:

> We just haven't enjoyed ourselves. We have had no time together. All we've done is raise kids. . . . So one thing that I know now is that one of the biggest problems was that I put the children first. I didn't put the marriage first or my husband. Now I can see that he's all I've got. My kids are not there [any longer] for me, after I've sacrificed and done everything for them. . . . They will be, I know, in my old age. But right now they're not there for me. . . . For the first time in twenty years, [Dwain and I] are close, and I feel — I feel like I really care about him as a person. I can see that he's the one that will support me and will help me. I just told him that it just makes me sick to think it took me twenty years before I ever learned to appreciate him. . . . We have taken time off together to be alone [now], whether we thought we should or not. We've just done it. We've gone down to Yosemite. We like to just go sight-seeing like that.

When couples fail to develop a new intimacy in these years, the problem is usually that they find they no longer have any common interests. They discover new time together in their fifties but have nothing to share in that time.

Mary, a successful fifty-two-year-old real-estate agent, is married to an unemployed alcoholic who has grown steadily less accessible to her over the years. Mary wiped away her tears as she spoke of a marriage that had become progressively devoid of passion and concern. As their children moved away from home, Mary found that only their concern for childraising had held her and her husband together. She concluded her painful interview by declaring that, "Without love, people die." Mary may soon face her own psychological death unless she can find a way to improve this marriage or extricate herself from it. Many men and women, like Mary, who face stagnation at this point in their life, will turn to people outside their marriage to fill their increased need for intimacy. Separation and divorce are often waiting in the wings.

We have little data from our interviews about the relationships of gay men and women in their fifties. With a continuing focus on youth in the gay male culture, many men in their fifties have not established long-term permanent relationships. "I attract them, but I don't keep them," Claudio stated. "I don't think that this is unique. I think that a very small percentage of homosexual men have lovers and keep them for any significant length of time. It's a way of life. As for right now, the emotional part of me says that I would like someone watching the fire burning in the fireplace. Then there is the other part of me that says it's a bit too late. There are other things that have to be done that are more important."

Another gay interviewee, Sam, a fifty-eight-year-old painter who lives communally with several gay and straight women and men, talked about his fear of intimacy, a major fact for many men in the gay culture that works against their forming long-term relationships. He felt that he had "seen too many people blow it. . . . I chose not to have a long [relationship]; I just don't want to get so close to people. Also, a family with children doesn't seem to work together with painting. . . . I've never had, nor do I desire a long-term relationship with another man." He laughed as he said, "I have a horrible image of shopping in Macy's on a Saturday, with a kid in a stroller!" For both these gay men, their friends serve as a surrogate family through whom intimacy is sought and often achieved. Through Claudio's best friend of some thirty-seven years, he was introduced to new friends who, he observes, "have opened up new doors for me. They are constantly opening up new doors — new ideas. That's how they affect me and my life. They have given me hope."

Gay men in their fifties who have stayed with a partner over a long period of time, move through the marital maze much like any heterosexual couple, seeking and achieving intimacy and caring. Also, as a result of the AIDS crisis, more gay men are searching for longer relationships and greater intimacy.

Some of the most important and intimate relationships gay men form are with women. The most important person in the life of the gay painter we interviewed, for example, is a heterosexual woman, also in her fifties, who is a poet and a painter. "She's a good confidante," he noted. "My most stable relationship. The phone has kept us together. We're able to exchange the 'big' things. She's like a surrogate sister." Among the gay and straight friends who have become his family some of the younger ones serve also as "surrogate kids."

Claire, a fifty-three-old hospital clerk, has been an active member of a religious gay and lesbian group and has been in a committed relationship for the last ten years with a woman who is one year older. Her original goal in life, Claire admitted, was to get married, have children and "live happily ever after." That traditional dream, however, turned out to be a disappointment — except for her twenty-seven-year-old son who is now in the Navy. "I can't imagine my life without him," Claire acknowledged. She continues also to have regular contact with her ex-husband, maintaining relationships from both her present and past life.

One Last Chance

Our intimate relationships in our fifties are sometimes affected by the feeling that we still have time for "one last chance at happiness." This can lead either to the breakup of an existing relationship or to a focus on maintaining and improving that relationship, reveling in the satisfaction and pleasure of having created and sustained a "good" marriage for example.

Conversely, for some men in their fifties, the idea of one last chance for happiness and a final fling at youth moves them to leave their "boring" wives for a younger woman. There are few of us in our fifties who have not witnessed this among our own circle. However, some wives find their marriages more gratifying during their fifties because their husbands become interested in exploring a more romantic and attentive role as part of their new orientation toward relationships, affiliation, and interdependence. These are often the women who can accept men in less traditionally "masculine" roles, as they themselves become comfortable with their own new interest in autonomy.

Karen, for instance, has been married three times, at ages twenty and thirty-six and in her mid forties. Her first marriage lasted thirteen years, the second only two years, but it is her third marriage that brought an intimacy that previously was lacking. Karen feels that there is much more interdependence in this marriage, while she personally has become less dependent on the relationship than she had been during her first two marriages. She sees Frederick, her third husband, as very supportive and sensitive. In her previous marriages, Karen (like many other women) had felt very much like a "mother" to her husbands. Now, even though Frederick is somewhat younger than Karen at thirty-nine, she allows and even encourages him to be nurturing and supportive, something she had not been able to do in her previous marriages. This shift, in turn, allows her to find and exhibit greater autonomy without jeopardizing the relationship.

Mary Anne, who is in a new relationship following the death of her husband three years ago, describes this relationship as being very different from her marriage. "Now I want someone to worry about me," she said, "to take care of me." Having raised six children, Mary Anne is now ready to move away from her mothering role. The man she is seeing is, at last, "somebody I can learn something from and I can enjoy."

As women take on greater responsibilities and interests outside the family, and men become more interested in close relationships, their paths can diverge, but in other cases, they may find they have come closer in their behavior. Margaret, for instance, describes both her husband and herself as becoming much more like each other. She finds herself "nicely assertive now, not hysterical like before, or [even] reactionary. Now I talk 'reasonable.'"

Alex made a similar discovery about his twenty-three-year relationship with his wife, Bev, which he describes as "solid and good. Of course we have our share of disagreements — well, fights — but we love each other very much. . . . Since our daughter left, we have been much closer, especially since [our daughter] was the source of many of our arguments. My wife is very caring and protective. [Now] she actually has become more independent in many ways and seems happier with this." When asked the primary reasons for Bev's new independence, Alex said that, in addition to their daughter's leaving home, "I think that moving to a small town forced us both to become more self-reliant. It is not exactly like some middle-size suburban city. I've encouraged her to pursue her interest, and she has really gotten into it. She has her full-time work—which she finds gratifying—and her friends and her family. She stays pretty busy. We enjoy our time together. Our relationship has sort of evolved into bringing us closer together. We have become better friends in recent years. There is more mutual respect."

Living in a Youth-Oriented Culture

Often, it is vanity and virility that create relationship crises for middle-age men. But why are these factors critical for some men and not for others? The answer may lie with the culture itself. We live in a youth-oriented culture. For men, youth, attractiveness, and athleticism are thought to translate into being magnetic in personal relationships, successful in work, and eternally envied and desired by others.[4] The object becomes to look young, act young, and think young. Whole industries, as Michael McGill points out, "have been built upon the pursuit of youth— cosmetics, clothing, cars. . . . One of the fastest growing industries in recent years . . . is the 'vanity insanity' for men—male cosmetics, designer styles for men, the fitness business. . . . Corporations and organizations of all sizes are evidencing increasing concern over the health and vitality of their executives. As often as not, this concern takes the form that the young man is better than the old man, the thin man is better than the fat man, the dark-haired man is better than the gray-haired man, the athletic man is better than the sedentary man, and so on.[5]

Both men and women, unable to ignore the promise of perpetual youth, can invest themselves fully in its pursuit. As he faces the physiological changes that accompany middle age, the typical fifty-year-old man responds in one of three ways:

he takes corrective action to reduce the threat (typically by adopting the appearance and behavior of youth), he removes himself from those things that remind him of his age, or he changes his behavior in such a way as to put down the threat, to attack it, or to prove that he is still young, vital, and virile.[6]

In their quest for eternal youth, women in their fifties may begin to dye their hair to hide any trace of gray. As "crow's feet" appear around their eyes and wrinkles in their faces and necks, they may turn to a plastic surgeon to have their eyes "done" or their faces lifted. As their body shape changes, they may choose loose clothes and store away straight skirts and dresses with cinched waistlines. Short shorts are replaced by culottes and skorts.

Inundated with health and fitness news, some men and women adopt a health or exercise regimen. They may not be committed to weekly aerobics class, but long walks and moderate hikes may begin to appear on their calendars even though their generation was not brought up to "get out there and sweat."

Cultural attitudes and fashions remind us daily — in both blatant and subtle ways — that the United States is indeed a youth-oriented society, yet each of us must choose those styles and activities with which he or she feels most comfortable. There is help on the horizon, however. As the number of people in their fifties grows with the surge of the baby boomers, being stylish in America may begin to include sporting gray hair and shorts.

Tolerance in Relationships

Typically, couples in their fifties who have lived with each other for many years have come to terms with the fact that their spouses are unlikely to change much in the future. They have learned to accept their partners' strengths and weaknesses. Paradoxically, for many of the fifty-year-olds in our study, this attitude of greater acceptance has led to some tangible changes in their marriages.

Suzanne, a fifty-one-year-old woman who had been married to her spouse, Ben, for thirty-one years, gave her marriage a high grade: "It is well worth it!" she glowed. But she admitted that this was not always the way she felt. For the first fifteen years, Suzanne and her husband had a "traditional marriage" in which Suzanne was responsible for child rearing, housework, finances, scheduling various appointments, and entertaining.

When the children were older, Suzanne and Ben began "to look at the quality of the marriage." Suzanne said that this was a "turbulent time" for both of them. She filed for divorce on three different occasions, and for a time, they separated. At that point in her life, Suzanne felt that she was responsible for Ben's happiness and that she had assumed the roles of "lover, friend, and mother" for her spouse. However, during their separation, Suzanne dated and found that she was attracted to men very similar to Ben. She made the decision that she would "rather be with the father of my children" than with a new man similar to her husband. She had come to accept the fact that Ben was "a wonderfully dependent male," but her acceptance made things change for her. Ben and Suzanne now share many household duties, and Suzanne no longer feels responsible for Ben's happiness. "I can't make him change," she noted. "I let go of the control. It was freeing."

Tolerance has become important to Gwen, too. Now in the midst of her third failed marriage, she wishes that she had married her high school boyfriend because "he really knew me and liked me in spite of it."

Relationships between men and women change for many reasons in this transitional fifties decade, but few avoid change of some kind. Comparatively few couples totally reverse roles, but most have experienced some role shifts. Sexuality does not usually diminish but rather leads to a new, enhanced intimacy and satisfaction. And, if the changes underway have not split the couple asunder, there is now a far greater acceptance of and welcome for each other's value and worth.

Intimate relationships tend to become more comfortable as individuals increase their knowledge of themselves and their partners and as they shift their priorities, focusing attention on those things that each of them really cares deeply about. At this time in life, generativity through redefining intimate relationships can be the keystone to reinvention for many men and women. It seems to be a risk worth taking.

Families:
New Roles as Parents,
Grandparents, and Children

When it was time to climb the stairs that night,
Dad went first, like he always did.
He put his right hand on the railing,
then dragged each stone foot up
in slow and strained, supremely careful moves.
And together we inched our way along.

As we climbed, I thought
of the pack trips we used to take.
He was in front then, too,
his strong, stocky legs guiding us
over smooth white passes
that held the sky like open hands.
He was in front then, too.

But now his legs were thin and weak,
dry sticks still clinging to the ancient oak.
Now his high country was a room one story up
where craggy ledges hung
in wooden picture frames
and plants and flowers grew in round red earthen pots.

So, to the room we climbed
And, as we did, I saw in his eyes
an evening calm.
This was not a time for tears, they said,
simply a time for less.

—*David Meuel*

Although most of us in our fifties are through with the pains and joys of actually raising children, more and more of our young adult children are remaining at home, or returning after brief periods of independence and living with us until they are in their twenties or even their thirties. There are many different reasons for this (the high cost of housing, the slowdown in the national economy, lengthened years of schooling, psychologically extended early adulthood, and delayed marriages or early marital breakups), but whatever the reason for any particular family, this unpredictable adult-child "boomerang" pattern in which young adults move back into their former rooms, use the phone, occupy the bathroom, recapture the television, and complicate the daily schedule often puts a strain on parents in their fifties.

To make the situation even more complex, some men and women in their fifties may also be grandparents. Thus, as we attempt to make sense of our life experiences from age fifty to sixty, we are simultaneously confronted with the task of ending an era of traditional parenting, sorting out the complexities of parenting our young adult children, and being grandparents to their young children. Finally, we are also often taking on new responsibilities for our own aging parents. This complex intergenerational picture has given rise to an appropriate phrase to describe the men and women in their fifties who are caught in the middle: the Sandwich Generation.

If I Could Do It over Again

During our fifties, our work as traditional parents is, for most of us, finished. Our children are grown, and most of us feel that there is not much more that we can do to influence their values, directions, or even aspirations at this late point. We must accept what we have done with our children and watch from the sidelines to see how things have worked out.

This time of life is often a source of real gratification as we watch our children flourish and, in many ways, become more like us. They no longer have their adolescent needs to be different from us in order to establish their own identities. We can feel vicarious gratification when we proudly witness their achievements. Though we ourselves may lack the energy "to leap tall buildings with a single bound," we can experience the particular thrill of watching our children accomplish this feat. We can also enjoy a sense of continuity, knowing that our values, skills, and aspirations have been passed on to the next generation.

When our relationship with our children as adults is working well, we share ideas. We listen to their dilemmas about work and career. We discuss politics. We help each other with business decisions. We confer about the color of the towels for their new homes and apartments. We deepen our friendships and reaffirm our caring for one another. Under the best of circumstances, our children affirm with their own lives all that we have taught them.

Frequently, our adult children gain a new sense of appreciation for our influence and commitment as parents. Many of the men and women we interviewed mentioned how this era in their lives was particularly gratifying for them as parents. One housewife and mother, Tobi, refers to her daughter-in-law as her best friend. Her daughter-in-law is an artist who has given priority, like Tobi, to "her mothering career." Tobi, who no doubt identifies with her daughter-in-law, is supportive of the younger woman and, in return, finds someone who listens.

We may also form close relationships with our sons- or daughters-in-law. While some popular myths and television's situation comedies portray strained or antagonistic relationships between in-laws, the men and women in our study spoke favorably about their relationships with their sons- and daughters-in-law and often admired their devotion or skills as parents.

On the negative side of the ledger, the fact that our fifties represent the end of the era in which we can influence the course of our children's development is a source of considerable frustration and pain for some. Some of us may want to do it all over again — with the advantage of our newly acquired wisdom and insight about the "real" values of life. This sense of lost opportunity was often expressed when the men and women in our study were asked what they would do differently in their lives. Most often they said that they would have liked to have had better relationships with their children.

Ted, for instance, feels that he has been a sincere and dedicated man and a faithful husband for almost forty years; however, he also feels partially responsible for his two sons' marital breakups. He is particularly disappointed about his youngest son, for he felt very involved with this child and wishes that he had intervened much earlier in his marriage. From the start, Ted felt that his son's wife was the wrong person for his son and that the marriage would end in divorce as it ultimately, and sadly, did.

Another father, Ben, identified his son, who has been heavily involved with drugs and has been in and out of jail, as the single failure in his life. Ben continues to agonize over what he feels is his share of the responsibility: "Something that I was lacking to do for him had him change to drugs and things. [I] didn't keep [him] out of it or pull him away from it."

Beatrice also describes having experienced "a lot of failures with my children" and particularly blames herself for many of the troubles experienced by her daughter: "I feel really bad about her and me, because I feel like, probably subconsciously, I took out on her the frustrations of being in a marriage that . . . I thought I didn't want to be in because of her. That I ended up marrying him because I felt guilty that she didn't have a father. So I went ahead and married. . . . But I look at all that we've been through, and it wasn't worth it. Except that you'd never know . . . maybe life would have been worse. I don't know. But I feel like my children — somehow I failed my children. I didn't give them the happy home life that they deserved."

Another woman, Karen, struggles with an even more profound loss. Her daughter, Susie, was killed in an accident at the age of eighteen. Karen continues to go back over her life as a parent, wondering if she did an adequate job as a mother for Susie, and like many parents who grieve the loss of their children, she questions whether there were ways in which she might have prevented Susie's death. There is an ancient Korean saying that one buries one's spouse in the ground but buries a dead child in one's heart. This never-ending process of grief may be heightened among men and women in their fifties as they confront the realization that their dead child might have given them grandchildren, and they feel even more sharply the incompleteness that such a major loss represents.[1]

Men and women in their fifties often indicate that they would like to have had more patience with their children and to have listened more carefully and caringly. Karen, for instance, has come to terms with her two surviving children. She wishes she had been more patient with them in their earlier years and is now firmly committed to being close, but "not intrusive," with her two sons. She remains busy with her own life and does not "rescue" either Brian or Perry. She lets them know that she is there for them, but wants them to have the space to do what they need to do.

When fifty-year-olds experience disappointment regarding their children, at the heart of their unhappiness is the wish that they had spent more time with the children. This was particularly true for many of the men we interviewed. Alex, for instance, who spoke of a rich relationship with his wife, also spoke of his failure to be more in tune with his wife and daughter earlier in his life and his failure in not spending more time with them when he was younger: "We had a good family. It could have been much better if I had put much more into it. I've learned to take the important things more seriously than I had before. Too many times my family took a back seat to my work."

Alex can at least partially make up for the time he lost with his wife, but he can never recover the time he lost with his daughter, who has now left home to start her own family. Alex laughed a little, then turned serious as he observed that his daughter "is getting older and more mature. I guess it makes me feel old just watching how fast she grew up and out. That is one of the mistakes that [I made], not spending enough time with her while she was home."

A painful absence of a meaningful parenting experience for fifty-year-old men is particularly prevalent in the United States. Men whom we interviewed from other Western cultures — including Hispanic, Italian, and Greek — often have had extensive close parenting experiences with their children. Similarly, many men from Asian cultures have had long, rich parenting experiences. Satis, a fifty-year-old man from India, emphasized his devotion to his immediate family, stating that his greatest success in life was "having met my wife and having two wonderful children." When his children were very young, Satis also accepted the role of the primary parent a substantial portion of the time, while his wife worked a swing shift. He also revealed, however, that "sometimes it bothers me a little bit to see my children grow up. They're more independent and don't need me or count on me as much as they used to."

Whatever their parenting experiences, fifty-year-old men and women find that they must come to terms with those experiences if they do not want to endlessly relive them.

Live-in Children

In some cases we will face a particularly difficult kind of parenting when our adult children continue to live at home or return home. In those few cases where the men and women we interviewed still had children living at home, there were almost always problems. Mary speaks of her twenty-year-old live-in daughter as someone who "doesn't want to hear the things I have to say, so I am withdrawing somewhat and letting her do things on her own. That's difficult for me, because I want to take care of her." Mary acknowledges that, at the heart of the matter, is her own need for control when her daughter lives at home, which is compounded by the problem of simultaneous separation and attachment that accompanies the maturation of any child.

Another woman, Sylvia, still struggles with her live-in son but for different reasons now than when he was a teenager. "One night he came in at 5:45 A.M., and it woke me up," she recalled. "He started to yell about my not needing to worry about him anymore. I wasn't worried. I was mad that his car had awakened me!"

Bernice Neugarten's notion that there inevitably are developmental crises when one is "out of time"[2] certainly applies to mature, live-in children. In this instance, it is the child who is seen to be out of step with society's expectations when he or she either fails to move away from home by age twenty-one or moves back home after a divorce or a financial setback. Today's parents typically do not know how to handle the situation and neither does the adult child. Mary's annoyance centered on the issue of control. Sylvia's anger was not about control but about having a routine disrupted. Her son, however, treated her anger as an issue of control and responded like an adolescent defying parental authority. Mother and son were reading from different scripts—in part because there are no socially-established scripts, or behavior patterns, for the live-in adult child or the fifty-year-old parent.

One successful script was described to us by a man whose daughter suffered business setbacks and a breakup with her live-in boyfriend and business partner. He invited his daughter, who was in her late twenties, to move back home until she recovered financially and emotionally. The young woman's brother helped her with the physical chores of moving. Over the next two years, the daughter took a series of jobs and paid off all her debts. When she secured a permanent position with a steady salary, benefits, and some promise for the future, she obtained her own home and picked up the pieces of her young-adult social life.

Her devoted father now takes pride in how the entire family rallied to support this young woman. He is also proud of her perseverance and moral integrity in fulfilling her prior financial obligations. Although there were some minor daily inconveniences when the parental household once again expanded, arrangements were adult for the most part, with each party maintaining his or her independence, schedules, and interests, much as before.

This family turned a potential crisis into an opportunity to demonstrate their loyalty to each other. Rather than focusing on the daughter's setbacks as failures, the family "went with the flow" and trusted that the daughter would learn from her errors and be stronger for them in the future.

Coming to Terms with Ourselves as Parents

How do we come to terms with the outcomes of our parenting? Surely we must come to recognize that our early dreams about how we would perform as parents were probably not realistic and, furthermore, belonged to another era.

As parents — and grandparents — we must somehow confront the fact that we are not now, nor have we ever been, the kinds of parents that our own mothers and fathers were. In some ways, we may be better parents. While some of our parents may have used harsh discipline or corporal punishment, we read Dr. Spock and learned to raise our children in a more reasoned and permissive manner. A touch more democracy was offered in our homes, and we held a bit more understanding in our hearts.

We also did things that may have made us less successful as parents. Most of us allowed (and even encouraged) our children to watch television on their own and develop personal interests, and we avoided the involvement that comes from sharing many stories and activities. Many of us probably spent too little time even on weekends with our children. The old family traditions of going on Saturday picnics or visiting relatives on Sunday or taking a Sunday drive seem to have died, and as modern parents, becoming forever busier, we have obviously helped to bury these traditions.

One way in which we can come to terms with ourselves as parents is by shifting the nature of our relationships with our adult children. The men and women we studied talked about progressing from parent to friend with their grown children. Now, they say, they can maturely discuss both personal and contemporary events together. They can thoroughly enjoy their children's companionship — their wit, knowledge, and wisdom. Betty, a fifty-three-year-old executive secretary, says, "I enjoy my relationship very much with my married daughters. [They] are very independent, and they don't seem to depend on me for approval, which is good, because I want them to be independent. . . . I have the relationship, I think, of a good friend with each of them. I relate to some better than others, but I feel like a good friend and somebody that they can enjoy being with. I enjoy being with them. They don't come to me for advice very often. And I don't give them advice unless they ask for it." Betty described her daughter, Grace, as her confidant.

Our children can now become important sources of support for us as we grapple with the increasing complexity of our own lives. We can expect them to return some of the caring attention we gave them as they were growing up. Our son can become "just like Dad," offering a comforting hug or a thoughtful word of encouragement. Our daughter can now appreciate her own mother, as she herself tries to fit her own "million things" into every busy day. Both parent and child gain new perspectives from these transformed relationships.

Our children are also likely to gain increased appreciation for us as they take on their own parenting responsibilities. We are all aware of the jokes about adult children coming to realize that their parents are not as stupid as they once thought they were (though parents will never again be as smart as they appeared to be to their very young children!).

Mary, the fifty-two-year-old real-estate agent with the alcoholic husband, has established a much needed supportive relationship with her daughter, Sarah, who now asks her mother for advice. During her rebellious adolescence, Sarah had contradicted virtually every idea that was presented by her mother. Mary noted that her daughter recently was "in a bit of a turmoil over a rental . . . so she's been calling me and she's treating me like a mother rather than an equal, and I rather like that. And I think she does too."

A final way in which we come to terms with the loss of the dependency of our children and with ourselves as parents is by moving on with our own lives. When our children leave home, we have more time to ourselves. We have more time for our wives, husbands, or lovers. We have more time for other things in life about which we care deeply — whether they are our careers, hobbies, community services, or special causes. We also often find ourselves with more available money, more space in the house, and more privacy with which to pursue those dreams from early adulthood that we once had to put aside because they had become "couldn't do's": painting, camping, playing or watching sports, traveling, going to the theater or concerts, writing, and visiting our friends.

We come to terms with the void caused by the absence of daily parenting by filling it with many other interests and activities. We can never completely fill the void until we have come to grips with the loss, and even grief, that is associated with a child's absence. But we shall often be most effective in dealing with it if we reinvent ourselves by turning to our newly emerging interests or reawakening our dormant ones.

Differences Between Men and Women as Parents

While many of the parenting themes that we have identified are relevant to both men and women, there are also several major differences in the ways men and women seem to experience the end of active daily parenting. Some of these gender differences contradict deeply held assumptions about the perspectives and concerns of men and women.

First, there has been a long-held assumption that women in their forties and fifties suffer from the "empty nest syndrome." Women, supposedly, are especially distressed about their children leaving home, since childrearing has often been the major focus of their lives.

It is true that many of the women in our study identified themselves first and foremost as mothers, while only a third of the men perceived their successes and failures in life primarily in terms of parenthood. For these women, the shift away from motherhood as their primary source of identity and meaning in life was often disorienting.

Beth, a fifty-year-old psychologist we interviewed, described recent communication problems she was having with her husband as arising from her "empty nest — my children growing up and [our need to reestablish] a relationship between the two of us. I have one child left that is sixteen years of age, who will be leaving in two years. Rather than stay home and worry about the empty nest, I have decided to reach out with an education and further my development as a human being. I think that, as a result, my husband and I are sometimes growing apart. But at other times, I see that we still have a lot in common with one another."

For many of the professional and well-educated women we interviewed, the empty nest has been the force that propelled them out of the home and into the world. As a result, it has also tended to estrange them from their husbands. Although some women and men find that their empty nest has enhanced their relationship with one another and has provided them with more time together, for others the empty nest has produced an empty home and an empty marriage.

Some women, however, appeared to have taken the empty nest in stride. Patricia, a fifty-two-year-old insurance broker, for instance, laughed as she described a recent incident in which she heard the footsteps of her dog on the kitchen floor for the first time: "I didn't know dogs had toenails until this dog walked across the linoleum. I'd never heard it because this house was always filled with kids and noise. I mean, their buddies were always over. There was always something going on!" Pat went on to declare that she loves her newfound independence. "I think I deserve this [independence]," even though she misses the turmoil and spirit of the adolescents.

However, while the empty nest may often be a problem for women, it is an even greater problem for men.[3] Contemporary women, such as Patricia and Beth, now have an opportunity to start new careers or increase their commitment of time and energy to existing ones. They truly enjoy becoming more actively engaged in the outside world. For these women, the absence of children is a mixed blessing. They miss the children, but they also relish their new freedom to pursue a career, community service, or a long-ignored avocation.

For many men, on the other hand, the empty nest is no blessing at all. They see it as pure hell. As we have illustrated, men often become much more affiliative and reflective as they enter their fifties. Less consumed by their own ambitions and careers, they want to spend more time at home with their families. But just as they come home to announce their decision to place the family higher on their priority list, their children are heading off to live their own independent lives while their wives are heading out to the office.

For men then, even more than for women, the end of the era of daily parenting is often accompanied by the sense of lost opportunity. Many of the men we interviewed expressed this sense of loss. They want another chance to parent but realize that it is too late. Fortunately, for some of these men, grandparenting provides at least a partial answer.

The more common regret for women was that they had sacrificed their own careers and personal time for so long to their mothering role. While none of the women in our study said that they would rather not have had children, they often suggested that they had "grown up in the wrong era." They see around them today younger women who have been able to build a career and raise children without sacrificing one for the other. Many U.S. women fifty and sixty years of age in the 1980s and 1990s made major sacrifices for their spouses and families, while observing in their late thirties and forties the emergence of a feminist perspective that challenged the wisdom, or even the necessity, of this sacrifice. They discovered that the role of housewife and mother was being assigned an ever lower status. Although the model of the superwoman who is able to "have it all" is giving way to a more realistic model of choices and options — with women (and to a limited extent, men) being told that it is acceptable to drop out of the work force or to job share with another for a while to raise preschool children — the damage has been profound. Middle-age women often read these myths of the superwoman and supermom as an indictment of their own life choices, while viewing the new life and career models for women as coming too late for their own use and well-being. Thus, as we try to understand the experiences of women in their fifties today we must remain aware of the sociocultural shifts regarding female roles, which came along often after these women's primary roles as wives and mothers had already been decided.

Women are now coming to understand that they may be able to "have it all," but not necessarily all at the same time. There is not a "one size fits all" sequence of roles that will work for everyone. School, career, marriage, children, work, family — all must be rejuggled, rebalanced, and reintegrated at each stage of life.[4]

There is in every crisis an invitation to explore and invent. Women and men in their fifties will find that the empty nest can be a new beginning as well as an end, if they choose to make it so.

The Joys of Grandparenting

For many married men and women in their fifties, this has been a decade of their children's weddings and the births of their first grandchildren, the start of a new generation within the family line. We have watched many of our friends anticipating the birth of their first grandchild, assisting their daughters in childbirth, holding infants for the first time in many years, and setting aside once important meetings and social events in order to baby-sit. Old memories of infant behaviors burst forth. Life-cycle rituals and baby-naming ceremonies reach deeply into long dormant familial and religious psyches. Prayers are heard from nonreligious mouths. Gifts are given abundantly without thought of "spoiling." Photographs and video cassettes capture each grandchild's weekly growth.

Many of the men and women in their fifties who had grandchildren spoke of grandparenting quite simply as an extraordinary experience. Veronica described a "red letter day" for her as one in which she takes her grandchildren to a nearby restaurant. Penelope gushed that grandmothering was "heavenly." And still another woman, Ruth, waxed ecstatic about her new role as grandmother. She sees her grandchildren frequently and says that they, in turn, idolize her.

For the men we interviewed, grandparenting is often judged to be a good deal more satisfying than parenting. Charlie describes his relationship with his three young grandchildren as "super." He feels great when he is with them and thinks they feel warm and happy when they are with him. Grandparenting, for Charlie, has all of the pluses and none of the minuses of his relationships with his own children.

Men in their fifties seem better equipped for parenting — and, as an extension, grandparenting — than they were during their thirties and forties when career advancement and achievement took precedence over family. They sometimes believe that as grandfathers they can make up, at least in part, for their neglect as parents. However, several men in our study also spoke sadly about the unexpected reactions of their children to their success and joy in grandparenting. "Why couldn't you have been as good a father as you are a grandfather?" was their children's main criticism. There is a sense of frustration and anger among some adult children as they witness the caring attitude of their fathers toward their own children. They may wonder, "Why couldn't I have had this kind of care?" Even now, as grown adults, they would like some of our attention.

Grandparenting may also be enjoyable because it seems to allow for detachment and fewer boundaries and responsibil-ities. In our study, many men and women discovered that they had levels of patience and playfulness with their grandchildren that they had not experienced with their own children. In part, their new patience may result from their own maturation and decreasing need to change and mold other people, especially members of their own families. The new playfulness may result from an emerging desire to return to a less responsible time. Grandparenting is certainly one of the best ways for those of us in our fifties to return to our perhaps submerged but not entirely lost childhoods.

Grandparents may also tend to be patient and playful because they do not have to live with their grandchildren day in and day out or assume the formal responsibilities for their upbringing. As one woman we interviewed said, "There is no responsibility. You can play and be friends. You can be nice all the time. I'm at my best. I think I'm a fun grandma. I like to act crazy and make the kids laugh!"

Katherine speaks of her "playful" grandparenting in similar terms, saying that her grandchildren are "delightful. I have a nice relationship with them, a very loving one. [I am] more relaxed and comfortable in dealing with my grandchildren than my own children because everything is not such a crisis anymore. The world will not come to an end if they stick their tongue out at me or if they say, 'I don't like you.'"

For women in their fifties, there are often additional joys in being a grandparent. Women often take particular delight in watching their own offspring assume the new and significant role of parenting. They suddenly begin to see the influence which they have had on their own children in new ways. Millie, for example, said with pride that "the biggest thing was watching my daughter taking care of the baby." When women observe their own sons and daughters raising their grandchildren in a manner that resembles their own parenting, they come to a quiet reassurance about their personal long-term impact. Millie finds that she also loves watching her husband feed their daughter's baby and that she herself also relishes feeding her new grand-daughter: "It was almost a meditation to feed her a bottle. I found it so very soothing, knowing that she wasn't mine and I didn't have the total responsibility."

As grandmothers, women often find they can enjoy time with their grandchildren while simultaneously investing in a career, avocation, or community service. In a sense, they have now found a way to "have it all." They can be both autonomous career women and nurturing grandparents.

The Problems of Grandparenting

For many women and for some men, however, there is pain as well as joy in grandparenting. A number of those we interviewed report that they live long distances from their grandchildren, thus minimizing any real sustained pleasure and interaction with them.

In addition to this barrier of distance, the complex lifestyle of a number of fifty-year-old grandparents is an impediment. At fifty-seven, Rebecca wants to establish a career after forty years of marriage and "being stuck at home with three children." Her children's families all live nearby, but she feels that she and her grandchildren haven't had a terribly close relationship, mainly because she has been working all the time. "It isn't a thing where I never wanted to be grandma," she explains, "but I'm not really the one who is baking the cookies and doing a lot of the crafts that [I might do] if I had more time. I think that maybe [then] we would have more fun."

Rebecca recalls that her own mother "certainly was the grandmother. Although she worked, we were close. She lived across the pasture. My children always went across to see grandmother. She was there. She did a lot of the baby-sitting. I miss that, and I wish I could baby-sit for my daughters but not everyday because I am working." For Rebecca, just as for many youn-

ger career-oriented parents of the 1990s, the pull between her
own work and childraising is a source of psychological strain —
even though the child raising role in question is grandparenting.

Barriers to grandparenting seem to prove particularly
painful for those men and women who feel that they did not
do a very good job of parenting and want to make up for this
deficiency by being terrific grandparents. "I have not only missed
my opportunity to raise my children," said one interviewee, "I
have now missed the opportunity to participate in the raising
of my grandchildren."

New Grandparenting Roles

A relatively new phenomenon that can further complicate the
grandparent role for men and women in their fifties occurs when
the grandparents are divorced. If each of them remarries, there
are essentially four grandparents on one side of the family con-
stellation. If both sets of grandparents divorce and remarry, the
grandparents grow to eight! This creates a high level of complexity for everyone, including the grandchildren. If there is ill-
will between the former husband and wife who are now grandparents, the situation becomes even more complicated. Who will
come to the grandchildren's birthday parties? Who will the
grandchildren consider to be their "real" grandparents? We will
not know the full effect of this form of extended family until
the children and grandchildren of these diverse families grow
into adulthood and begin to tell their own stories and explain
the effects of others' decisions on their lives.

Another complex aspect of grandparenting for today's men
and women in their fifties occurs when their children divorce.
Child custody cases involving "grandparents' rights" have become more common. Also, as increasing numbers of women,
and men, become single parents, grandparents often come to
play a more primary nurturing role for their grandchildren than
they might have anticipated.

Relatively young grandparents in their fifties can often
find themselves bringing up yet another generation of children.
Although this second generation role may be welcomed by some,
for others a new round of responsibilities for young children

may be an unwelcome burden, robbing the grandparents of a period of life that they had anticipated would be free from new responsibilities.

Today's grandparents must also be prepared to deal with the changing values and life-styles of contemporary young adults. When Lisa, a successful attorney, announced that she was pregnant and intended to keep her child although she was not married, her mother and stepfather were shocked. Even though her mother's life had included multiple marriages, due to both divorce and the early death of one of her three husbands, having a child out of wedlock had been out of the question in her day. It took many months for Lisa's mother to accept her role as a grandmother and to learn how to support her daughter's conscious decision to become a single mother. By the time this grandchild was a toddler, she was just beginning to experience having grandparents—and the grandparents were just beginning to accept the child as one of their own.

Another complex grandparenting role is required when a son or daughter adopts a child. When an infertile couple adopts a child, it is commonly viewed as a positive event. The grandparents typically celebrate and wholeheartedly accept the adopted grandchild as their own, just as do the adoptive parents. But when an adoption is more complex—involving racial differences, disability, surrogate parenthood, single parenthood, or a gay couple—the grandparents may often have ambivalent feelings toward the adopted child. As these once rare events become more commonplace, the grandparenting roles of people in their fifties increase the complexity of life—just at a time when most men and women are seeking to simplify their lives.

Surrogate Grandparenting

For men and women in their fifties who have remained childless by choice or circumstance, natural grandparenting is out of the question. Today's increasing numbers of childless women are likely to find a void in their lives in their later years, unless they become involved with others' children in some way. Assuming a surrogate grandparenting role in their later years is a source of pleasure and generativity for many childless women.

Some "maiden aunts" and "bachelor uncles," as they used to be known, find ways to stay involved in family activities and relationships even though they do not have children of their own. In some cases, when a great-niece's or great-nephew's real grandfather dies or divorces, uncles take over the grandfather role in place of the brothers. Becoming a surrogate grandfather can enrich the later years of many bachelors and reconnect them to the family. Similarly, great-aunts can take on grandmothers' roles.

These many new, evolving roles and relationships will start to be more common and visible in the decade ahead. Along with widening life-style options come new forms of family. Little research now exists on these new patterns, and they are fertile areas for further investigation.

Culmination and Generativity

According to our study, it seems important for many men and women in their fifties to find whatever ways they can to be with their grandchildren and to establish new forms of the traditional extended family. For men, in particular, their fifties may prove to be their most important decade for the kind of life enrichment associated with the care and raising of children. For women, their fifties may be the most important decade for the kind of life enrichment associated with passing on the values and the norms of daily living to yet another generation.

One serious concern for some grandparents in their fifties is their continuing relationships with their own children. In some cases, as noted earlier, they report that their own children seem jealous about the attention they are now devoting to their grandchildren. As one adult child was reported to have said to a parent, "I wish I could have gotten the attention from you that you are devoting to [my child]!"

Other grandparents report they feel much freer in relating to their grandchildren when the children's mom or dad is absent. As one woman noted, "I like [my grandchildren] best when I can have them to myself without their mother being there, because I feel like, one-on-one, I can get closer to them."

Finally, some fifty-year-olds do feel that the attention

grandparenting requires is too demanding. For example, Frieda feels that she has a good relationship with her grandchildren; however, both she and her husband sometimes find it exhausting to keep up with the changes that youngsters inevitably go through. "There was a time," she observed, "when Kristine [one of her grandchildren] wanted all kinds of attention from her grandparents, especially Grandpa. Then [inexplicably] she didn't want any attention from her grandparents!" Frieda realizes that this is only a stage that children go through, but the swings between wanting and not wanting attention take their toll. When Kristine was going through this stage of wanting to be left alone, she wouldn't even talk to her grandfather.

Another grandparent, Arlene, is struggling with menopause as well as with mixed feelings about caring for an ailing mother. She is just as ambivalent about her grandparenting role as Frieda. Initially, she spoke with great joy about her grandchildren, expressing how much pleasure and fun there was having her grandchildren at her home, working together on art projects, or taking hikes, or sending them off on camping trips with Grandpa. When the grandchildren ride in the car with their parents or their grandfather, Arlene organizes games, books, and projects for them to do: "I am the nursery school teacher type, who always has projects for the kids. They just came back from [a movie] with their grandpa. They had the most wonderful time, and Fred [her husband] says, 'I am so glad you had these projects, because if we were traveling, they would have driven us crazy.' We try to always, always have projects." However, the numerous projects and meals that she now organizes for her children and grandchildren also remind her of earlier pressures of parenting, thus reintroducing a real ambivalence about being in the traditionally feminine caregiver role.

Grandparenting seems to be viewed as a rewarding experience by the men and women we interviewed only when done in occasional doses. Otherwise, it reminds them too much of their earlier parenting roles, which were seen as restrictive and not always enjoyable or rewarding. Nevertheless, most of our grandparents appreciated that grandparenting can have a lot of pluses with just a sprinkling of minuses.

Moreover, grandparenting is a culmination, for it is an affirmation of the continuation of the family line and, therefore, of one's own existence. It is a culmination because, in the grand-parenting role, one has a second chance at the parenting role. This second chance can allow men and women to be different kinds of parents, less restrictive and more fun-loving, based on both life experience and a special freedom from ultimate respon-sibility. Our children now begin to model what we taught them and what we ourselves often were taught by our own parents long ago. While technology has added new conveniences and gadgets to the task, the ultimate fundamental bond of human nurturing that is restored to our lives through grandparenting in our fifties remains the same. The life cycle is reaffirmed.

As endings are often new beginnings, so grandparenting is both culminating and regenerating. The end of childhood for our own children becomes the beginning of childhood for our grandchildren. The birth of a new generation gives us literal generativity.

This core theme of our fifties — culmination leading to generativity — is a theme that we see repeated in all areas of our lives during our fifties. Grandparenting is only one aspect of this continuing cycle of life — an aspect of the relationships with others that often lead to the reinvention of self and generativity in our fifties.

Relating to Our Aging Parents: A Reversal of Roles

Caring for an elderly parent or confronting the death of one or both parents is a major task for many men and women who have entered their fifties. A number of writers and psycholo-gists have remarked on the critical transition that occurs in the developmental process of many adults when their parents die.[5] Of greatest importance is the often abrupt recognition that it is we who are now the senior generation. We suddenly find that we no longer have someone to look toward for guidance and authority. There is something extraordinarily profound about the ultimate sense of responsibility that we assume when there is suddenly no one else "running interference" in our family or in our organization.

Among the women we interviewed, Emily speaks of having been "in a low-grade depressed state" for several years following her father's death. Others describe their anger about parents dying without a mutual resolution of long-standing disagreements. Even when our parents have been mainly a source of contention and counterargument over the years, their loss is still felt keenly, for a new identity must be forged if there is no longer any parent against whom to exert our personal will. As an alternative to finding this new identity, many will continue the battle against the parent in their minds, just as some will continue to unconsciously seek the respect of a parent who is no longer alive. Still, there is a major difference for most adults between rebelling against or trying to please a real person and rebelling against or trying to please a legacy from the past.

Men and women in their fifties who still have living parents often must care for a dying or infirm mother or father. As we mentioned earlier, at fifty-four, Alex is wrestling with three significant relationships. He is trying to establish a closer relationship with his own wife; he is grappling with the growing infirmities of his elderly mother; and because of these demands, he feels that he is losing an opportunity to spend valuable and limited time with his daughter. However, he seems also to have come to terms with the fact that he, not his sisters, will continue to be the primary caregiver for his mother: "She lives in a senior housing complex that she really likes. It is one of those minimal care facilities where folks can live as independently as they'd like but have the support services when they need them. My mom is doing pretty well for someone who is seventy-seven years old. I have always been pretty close to my mom, and I feel primarily responsible for her at this time. My sisters help out, but the distance makes it impossible for them to be around when Mom really needs something."

Alex is fortunate in being able to help his mother yet not having to live with her on a daily basis, as do many men and women in less affluent circumstances. He is also fortunate in having been able to accept his role. Many of the men and women we interviewed quarrel with their brothers and sisters about the appropriate amount of responsibility (whether represented by time, money, physical presence, or decision-making authority) that each sibling should assume for aging parents.

When asked about ways in which his relationship with his mother has changed over the past few years, Alex observed that "now I am more the parent to her than she is to me. [However], she still chews me out and offers lots of parental advice, [whether I] like it or not. We have a very close relationship. She had a coronary bypass operation two years ago, and I realized then that I wouldn't always have her around. She has done well since the operation, but because of her age, I worry a great deal about her. My wife and my mom are very close and that has always helped." Like many other participants in our study, Alex still receives a healthy dose of advice from his living parent, even though the advice may no longer be appropriate nor backed up with any real authority.

As Alex also says, though, he is becoming his mother's "parent." Men and women in their fifties who find themselves serving as a respected source of advice for their aging parents are often disconcerted by it. Len and his wife, Deborah, for instance, spend considerable time with both their parents and often find themselves asked to provide guidance. They even make important decisions for their parents, but this reversal of parental roles is something about which they still do not feel comfortable.

One of the authors recently experienced this same disconcerting transition from advice-receiver to advice-giver. His father died unexpectedly several years ago, leaving his mother alone to manage their investments and to handle the family's other finances. Both of his siblings live in other parts of the United States, and as the youngest child, he was usually considered by his parents to be the least practical and most idealistic. Yet, now, he is the child closest to his mother. Having become a successful businessman, he finds himself sitting somewhat uncomfortably next to his mother in the chair formerly occupied by his father, while providing advice to her on financial matters. There are some profound questions that keep coming up for him: "When will mother begin to treat me as a child as she once used to? I don't enjoy this. This is really too responsible a position for me. And what would my father say? Would he approve of my advice now? Can I really fill his shoes?" Such insecurity and uncertainty about changing responsibilities is real for many of us in our fifties.

Arlene identifies still another source of ambivalent feelings when speaking of her commitment to provide care for her mother. "Women," she notes, "are [natural] caregivers. If you don't [care for others], you feel so guilty. . . . You want to be everything for everybody. This is the hard part." Whereas her mother had been selfless when young, devoting all her time and attention to other people, Arlene is aware of her own needs for time and space to herself. "My mother never changes," she observed. "I have to change." Yet her sense of responsibility for her mother, who made a sacrifice of self to provide for her daughter when she herself was young, is stronger than her own commitment to autonomy. Arlene feels she must provide the care that her mother asks of her.

Many fifty- to sixty-year-old men and women like Alex, simultaneously dealing with several important relationships have a full agenda to meet everyday. The central relationships in their lives all demand attention, while their inner voices concerning mortality and priorities in life make these relationships even more poignant and complex. Fortunately, Alex still has time to recover some of his lost opportunities with both his mother and wife. Building a relationship with his daughter may not be easy since she has already left home, but even here, he may be able to establish a new, richer relationship, so that neither he nor his daughter will face regret at that point in his life when she, in turn, must be prepared to care for him. Other men and women whom we interviewed were regrettably much less fortunate and wise. These people waited until after the deaths of their parents to confront their own neglectful or angry attitudes toward the parents. For these men and women, the decade of their fifties is often filled with grief and regret.

The Extended Family — Myth and Reality

With their calendars filled with new activities and involvements, people in their fifties often have little time for frequent meetings with other members of their families—whether they be brothers, sisters, aunts, uncles, or cousins—to develop a real support network. Spending time with family members has ceased to be a priority for most of us, and the days of the extended family are virtually gone from mainstream U.S. culture. Some of the men and women interviewed regard their separation from other family members with relief, feeling more negative than positive about past encounters with them. Others mourn the loss of those relationships. Still others find that the traditions of the extended family, especially when expressed through religious or ethnic rituals and celebrations, add a dimension of joy and connectedness not found anywhere else in their lives.

Betty, for one, speaks of losing contact with her family as her greatest failure in life. She accuses herself of giving her brothers and sisters only minimal attention. She tearfully admits that, as a result, "perhaps they don't realize how much I love them and care about them. But I have set my priorities in my life and have given the bulk of my time to my own children and husband." Unless people such as Betty discover how to resolve the problem of conflicting primary and extended family responsibilities, it will have an enduring impact on their own development.

Many men and women in their fifties who moved away from family members at an earlier stage in their lives make a new level of connection with aging family members a high priority as the years pass and older family members begin to die. Those who remain become even more precious and provide a link with our own parents and past generations that takes on new meaning as we ourselves age. On one level a sentimental attachment to the past, on another level this searching out of remaining family members strengthens our sense of our roots and continuity in the midst of a highly mobile society.

Household items that were special to us as children are remembered when visits to relatives take on the character of oral history sessions. Photographs long since forgotten are gathered up and displayed, as if to reassure ourselves that we really did belong to a larger family at one time. Personal items, often jewelry, may be accepted as a special gift while an aging relative is alive, instead of being inherited after his or her death. Sometimes gifts are returned to the givers by relatives sensing their own imminent deaths, or gifts may be left to the original givers in a will.

It is ironic that, as our own parents, grandparents, aunts, uncles, siblings, and cousins die and the extended family we knew best begins to shrink, our responsibility to convene the younger family members and their children becomes more apparent to us. Men and women in their fifties must then wrestle with whether or not they will take on yet another new role, that of family convener and keeper of the family's history, once viewed as the role of their parents. And so the cycle is repeated, and families continue to exist and to frame the major events of a lifetime: procreation, birth, and death.

Surrogate Extended Families

As the mobility of our society continues to increase and childlessness and divorce become more common, many family units shrink and function on a daily basis in very small groups. Many single adults and small family groups living away from other relatives, consciously create new extended or surrogate families among their friends.

In one suburban community, a group of families began a series of potluck holiday dinners more than thirty years ago. As the children in these families have grown up together, married, and become parents themselves, they have retained deep connections, reminiscent of many cousin relationships of past generations.

Typically, because women in our society live longer than men, the fathers of these men and women, who are now in their fifties, have died. The extended family of friends now includes an assortment of long-lived elderly mothers in their eighties and nineties, their children, grandchildren, and great-grandchildren. Four generations are now present at holiday dinners. For those whose own parents have died, the white-haired, maternal elders provide connections with a fading generation and give these friends many opportunities to show small kindnesses that they would have liked to shower on their own parents, now gone. A new kind of extended family, rooted in friendships, endures, and surrogate relationships enrich the lives of multiple generations.

This kind of reinvention of the extended family can offer a new kind of relatedness. It can provide the purposeful intergenerational creativity that gives men and women in their fifties — and the other members of their families — added resources, strengths, and sources of wisdom that are lost when people function autonomously. Creative efforts to retain and nurture new family-like groups can provide opportunities for generativity through connection, even as our own families move away and our aging parents die, leaving relationship gaps in our lives.

8

Work and Career:
Changing Needs
and Sources of Meaning

Whether you believe you can or believe you can't, either way you are right.

—Henry Ford

Men and women in their fifties structure their relationships to the outer worlds of work and career, leadership, and social and political activities in a number of different ways. However, many face a common set of questions: Do I have sufficient energy, patience, and commitment to give my work one more final push or should I leave it for younger men and women to carry on? How will I feel if others receive the credit for my accomplishment? How can I genuinely become a mentor for others and give away all that I have learned?

To see how fifty- to sixty-year-old men and women answer these questions we will look at their views of the meaning of work and career, the nature of authority and leadership, the shifts in social and political values and attitudes, and the nature of career and work achievement and failure. We will also explore gender differences that affect work and career and community leadership.

The first of these themes—the meaning of work and career—is the primary concern of this chapter. The other themes will be addressed more fully in Chapters Nine and Ten.

Patterns in Different Occupations

Men and women whose work has been dependent on their physical well-being and strength have passed their peak in their jobs by the time they reach their fifties and few of them continue to perform heavy physical work for long. However, in trades that require manual dexterity rather than physical strength, both men and women continue to perform well into their fifties and beyond.

In work that relies primarily on intellectual competence, we often find that men and women in their fifties begin to rely on their younger colleagues to carry the day-to-day work load, while they lend mature judgment and experience as mentors and supervisors. This is especially true in such professions as medicine, law, dentistry, management, and education. Today, lengthy professional experience and maturity must be balanced with up-to-date technical expertise in order to sustain high-quality professional practice.

In contrast to those engaged in physical trades, professional men and women in their fifties and sixties are often at the peak of their potential for assuming formal leadership tasks. They are often assigned roles that command respect and authority and that relate to the overall direction and operation of their corporations, human service agencies, and governmental organizations. But their informal influence and authority may actually have begun to decline. It is often the younger men and women in an organization who start running the show, even though the fifty-year-old leader and mentor is formally in charge and maintains positional leadership. However, many fifty- to sixty-year-old men and women now find themselves in positions to see their accumulated life's work finally have an impact.

Motivations for Work

By the time we reach our fifties, our reasons for working and establishing a certain kind of career usually are clear, although those reasons have often shifted from the time we first entered the work force, whether that was in our late teens, early twenties, or in our thirties or forties.

Men and women have usually had different patterns of entry and reentry to the work force. Most men's careers still show a linear pattern of work in one career—or at least in one field—throughout their lives, with a possible change of career in their forties or fifties. Although this one-career-for-life pattern is rapidly changing, it is still the prevailing model.

Women's patterns are more varied, with work outside the home often interrupted by periods of childbearing and childrearing that can range from a few weeks of maternity leave to an absence from the work force for more than twenty years. Many women reentering the paid work force in mid and later life have had to start all over again, often shifting fields or jobs many times in order to find fulfillment, earn more money, be promoted, or find challenging areas of interest.

For some of the people interviewed, work in itself is exciting and a source of substantial gratification. Karen describes work as "a kind of therapy for me." She recalls that her father always pushed her to work when she was "down." Devoting her energies to work has always made her feel better. Jerry similarly works in order to feel better. He worries, though, about being a workaholic in his job as a probation officer: "I'm not sure if it's what I really need to do, but it's what I like to do, and I do it well." Like many other men his age, Jerry has finally reached a point in his career where he commands respect and has some authority. He doesn't want to relinquish this long sought after phase of his career.

Claudio, a gay publishing executive turned teacher, recently retired from his second career of teaching to better deal with his life while coping with AIDS. He says that his Italian immigrant parents and Catholic school teachers imbued him with a strong work ethic:

> I was very much influenced as a small boy . . . by being a Depression baby born of immigrant parents. The work ethic was what I grew up under. The principles that were taught to me came from a rigid Catholic boys' school and from parents who got you up early in the morning. You were on a schedule, day in and day out. Summers were filled

with summer activities: camp, music lessons, reading. You didn't sit and loll around like today's kids do. You didn't ask for things until you were given them! I think, looking back, that I had a good childhood, but as I came into the 1950s and I came to New York, I went to college extremely influenced by [the idea of] becoming a success. . . .

We were the poor immigrants — relatively poor. I guess that we weren't really poor but were always told that we were poor, even with maids working around! I would say that it's a fear — an inbred fear — that is no different from the fear that 99 percent of my fellow Americans carry with them: a fear of walking away from that paycheck, from the material things.

This lingering fear and the realization that his continuing wellness has made it possible to work have led Claudio back into part-time teaching. His concern for security makes him regret his earlier retirement from full-time teaching and its attendant financial benefits.

Bob is similarly committed to his job and has become something of a workaholic. He looks at forced retirement with anger and observes that, in the United States, "it is wrong to get old. You [end up using] skin creams and hair dyes. What [the organizations] do is put you in a box, and the government backs them up." For Bob, work is an affirmation that he is still young and vital, that he is still being taken seriously, and that he is not yet an old man.

In our society, as in many others, work is central to identity, status, and economic well-being. "What you are" is often defined by "what you do." A common get-acquainted query at many a party is, "What do you do?" For many years, women now in their fifties have found this question threatening and destabilizing. Those who did not work outside the home tended to reply, "Oh, I'm just a housewife." Those who held a low-status job found some way to avoid an honest response.

Over the past few decades, work and the status connected

with it have occupied a central position in women's consciousness. Most "women's issues" — self-fulfillment, goal-setting, education, training, pay equity, participation in the military, social security inadequacies, child support, and so on — are rooted
in the changing nature of women's work roles. While some
women are fortunate enough to be able to choose careers primarily for self-fulfillment, most women who work outside the home
must do so primarily for economic reasons. Their income has
become essential to support themselves and their families.

Women's work at home — primarily childrearing and
housekeeping — is unrecognized and unpaid, but it is nonetheless work. The full-time homemaking and mothering role, although often denigrated because of its low social status, can be
meaningful and satisfying for many women — if it is also afford-
able. In the 1990s, we have begun to see increasing numbers
of professional and managerial women putting hard-won careers
on hold until their children are in school or on their way to self-
sufficiency, or because contemporary organizations are so stressful and unkind that the women choose to leave them.

Perhaps the most profound future influences on both men's
and women's motivations for work will be the results of new
technologies, especially in telecommunications. It is now possible to work with others all across the globe right from home.
As increasing numbers of people realize the potential of computers, modems, faxes, telephones, and other communication
technologies — and as further technologies are developed — dis-
tinctions between working at home and elsewhere will gradually disappear. While people's deep needs to physically meet and
affiliate with others may temper the speed and degree of this
transition and while face-to-face meetings and committee or conference work will occasionally be needed, in the future there
will be fewer reasons for men and women to join the worsening
commuter traffic. Moms and dads can thus tend to their children while also working on business deals, professional services,
or independent consulting projects. Even now, some kinds of
production workers have already returned to home-based con-
signments and crafts.

Such a shift in the workplace will also bring with it some

unforeseen problems. Are people who work at home to be considered official employees of the organization or outside contrac-
tors? What happens to pensions, retirement funds, medical and
insurance benefits, and sick or vacation days with full pay? How
will such workers meet their children's day care needs when these
new professionals get summoned to the central office for a staff
meeting or conference? These and other implications of such
a rearrangement must be given high priority if this future re-
orientation is to succeed. Not everyone, unfortunately, will find
such new freedom a blessing or even feasible. Nonetheless, further rapid and profound changes in the workplace are likely to
redefine both men's and women's motivations and ways of working in the decades ahead.

New Learning and Challenge Through Work

Many fifty-year-old men and women find intrinsic value in their
work because it is a source of new learning and challenge. Kyle
is a longtime tradesman in the printing industry who was born
in England and came to the United States at age twenty-six.
He has been with his company for twenty-five years and was
promoted to his managerial position only three years ago. He
speaks eloquently of the value he assigns to the learning he associates with his trade:

> I have come through the printing industry, from
> apprentice to journeyman, learning the trade and
> going through the changes we have experienced in
> the industry. It's been quite an experience. It has
> also been a rewarding experience. But my success
> was moving through the management part of the
> job, and this has been most rewarding to me. It
> certainly broadened my scope, and being part of
> the challenges of the future has been a great les-
> son. . . . I'm where I am today because of the way
> I do my job, and I feel I have been recognized for
> that. This job is a continuing learning process. I
> don't happen to think that, just because I have this

job, I have reached the goal I set for myself in life.
I feel that there is a lot more for me to do and still
a lot for me to learn.

Marsha also views her work as an actress primarily in terms of the personal growth that it provides her. She has been divorced for more than a decade and has raised two children as a single parent. She performs on stage and in commercials, not primarily to make money or become famous, but because she views acting as an ongoing challenge and source of significant personal learning. As she enters the second half of her fifties, Marsha wants to add yet another dimension to her performing arts career by returning to dance, which was her great love when she was a teenager. Neither acting nor dancing will provide financial stability, and she will probably continue to share an apartment with a friend. While her lack of funds prevents her from frequently visiting her grandchildren, who are located on the opposite coast, Marsha feels that she has good relationships with her children and grandchildren and that she is setting an excellent example for them as they select their own life goals.

Many fifty- to sixty-year-olds are less fortunate. They find that their work with various organizations, in and of itself, is not very rewarding. They seem generally bored, having done the same work for the past ten to twenty years. They complain of burnout, feel unappreciated, and are tired of working in dehumanizing and inequitable settings. Often, their views are no longer solicited, and they have been supplanted by younger, more "up-to-date" members of the organization. These older men and women tend to view their work and careers instrumentally, as a means to some other end — usually money and security — rather than as ends in themselves.

For these men and women, work has never been seen as a source of new learning and challenge. It was required but not expected to be enjoyed, and throughout their working lives, they have looked for ways to avoid work as much as possible and have sought challenge elsewhere. This is the TGIF, or Thank God It's Friday, crowd. Their vulnerability to stagnation is very real if they do not find alternative arenas to give them generativity. As their financial concerns rise along with the cost of living, while their potential for increased earnings flattens or decreases, their thoughts increasingly turn to how they might maintain financial security after retirement. They often begin to mark time and become less productive, resulting in their work roles becoming less important to their employers. This makes them more vulnerable to layoffs or early retirement. As a result, their stress and anxiety about future work is increased and their productivity may drop further, creating a vicious circle of worry and low productivity. Stagnation at this point is a real possibility, and their feelings of being stuck in their careers are rooted in reality.

Those more fortunate men and women for whom work and career continue to be major sources of generativity create positive circles in which learning and challenge lead to greater generativity and satisfaction that then leads to more learning and challenge. They return to school, enter training programs, or enroll in workshops and seminars to keep up-to-date in their current fields or to change careers altogether. They welcome new assignments and projects. When they leave the security of their corporate jobs and strike out on their own, it may appear that they have changed careers, but the shift of setting does not mean that their work itself has really changed. For men and women who work in areas they truly care about, work and career are implicitly bound up with the central meaning of their lives.

Work as Security

Many of those interviewed for this book conceived of work, at this point in their lives, as being primarily a source of financial support for themselves and their families. Satis, for instance, whom we met earlier, came to the United States from India more than thirty years ago when he was twenty-one. Six months before he was interviewed, he had lost a civil service job because of budget cutbacks. He had enjoyed this job only because it involved getting out of the office and provided him with welcome human contact. Totally devoted to his wife and two children, Satis works exclusively to provide financial support for them and sees one of his greatest failures as "not having been able to love my job, to find a job that I love." He now puts up with a great deal of stress in his new employment and has been geographically separated from his family for six months while they try to sell their old home. He remains in this job because "working to support [my family] has given me a meaning in my life."

Satis also felt that he had regressed spiritually by buying into the American dream. Now, not only does he work primarily for the money, he has come to like material things more. He says, "I used to feel more spiritual [in India], because of my environment. I had no money and less independence. [Instead, I had] community rootedness. The spiritual values are not the same here: there isn't any one way to live but rather many different ways."

Asked why he would not choose to go back to India, Satis said, "Because I'd feel like an old man there. In India people retire at fifty-five. They are old men there. Here, you're old [only] at seventy." While staying young is not an obsession for him, Satis jogs five miles three times a week and often plays tennis. When he returned to India on a recent visit, his family and friends thought it peculiar that he would jog at his age.

Other men and women in their fifties speak less about the funds they need at the present time to support their families and more about the money they will need to retire. Indeed, their immediate financial burdens are often reduced at this age, for their children have completed school and are living independently, and the mortgages on their homes are now low or paid off. But even though many fifty-year-olds would love to abandon their current jobs and strike out on their own, or at least find a more friendly and supportive place in which to work, they find themselves restrained by "golden handcuffs" in the form of medical benefits, vested retirement plans, or profit-sharing systems that force them to stay with their present organization until their scheduled retirement in their sixties in order to cash in fully. Even those without such benefits often stay in disagreeable jobs in order to build up their own independent retirement savings plans.

Like many modern-day fifty-year-olds we interviewed, Sandra, a suburban housewife, fears that she and her husband,

Len, may not have enough money to live on when they retire. She has already experienced bankruptcy once in her life and had to run from her creditors for a period of several years. She and her husband now own a contracting business and are always fearful of losing their savings. Furthermore, Sandra's husband has developed diabetes, making her fear that they will again "fall hard" and not be able to recover. Work is essential for Sandra and her husband if they are to build a nest egg for their old age. "I work really hard," Sandra noted. "I have a very demanding position in the school district. I guess I have a lot of influence, too. But I don't really enjoy it, and I seem to be getting more and more tired. Still, I need to go on working." They have had to make some difficult decisions. They have had to cut off financial support for one of their sons, who is struggling with a drug habit. Their active social life has been abandoned in favor of a more cautious and confining life-style. Sandra believes that nothing in life is certain, that she cannot count on anything but her own hard work. Even though their mortgage will be paid off in another three months, Sandra plans to continue working at her current job, which she truly doesn't like, until she is at least sixty-five years old.

Len, on the other hand, is somewhat more optimistic about his financial future and the financial stability of his family. Len is deeply religious and believes that he ultimately will be provided for by God and his church community. He still works at a boring job, however, to realize his dream of enjoying a rich, carefree retirement. In order to deal with the boredom, Len daydreams about doing new things after retirement. He feels that he has already started a "selective disengagement" from his current job and its related commitments. He would like to teach and write after retirement and is saving up money during his fifties to be able to pursue these activities without regard for salary or other forms of income.

Len, Sandra, and many other men and women in their fifties appear to be putting up with their current jobs because retirement seems to be just around the corner. Our society still tends to encourage this perspective, even though retirement in our postmodern world is not just around the corner for those in their fifties. In most cases, men and women will be working until age sixty-five before retiring. Problems now being faced by the federal government in sustaining a social security system that will remain financially viable may make it imperative for many men and women to remain employed up to age seventy and even beyond. How will people cope with an additional ten to twenty years of work in unrewarding or stressful jobs?

To answer this question, we have to ask another question: Is it really necessary for us to begin making decisions so early about our retirement? Is it really necessary for us to sacrifice these vital years by staying in unnourishing professions and jobs in order to be comfortably secure later in life? When do we stop sacrificing? When does the time come for us to cease deferring gratification for the future and begin actually living this fabled future?

An alternative to sacrifice is to find work that is an important end in and of itself. Many young women are seeking work today that has intrinsic meaning, as well as economic advantages; a growing number of men are also beginning to take this view.

Work as Community

Some fifty-year-old men and women value work primarily for the companionship and camaraderie that it provides. Many in our age group grew up in close-knit communities and families, establishing trusting relationships with their neighbors in small towns, city enclaves, or suburbs. Today, however, most of us can't seem to find enough time to meet and form friendships with our neighbors, especially when we commute long distances to work and are in two-career families. As a result, the friendships and the sense of community we form at work may be our new "neighborhood," filling the void left by the absence of community and extended family.[1]

Val typifies this perspective of work as community. She opened her own business twelve years ago and now employs eight women. According to Val, this business operates like a large family. "Some of these [women] have worked for me for ten to twelve years," she noted. "They all had their kids and families while they worked for me. I was an auntie to all of their kids." Her sense of community in her daily work environment seemed to be what was most important to Val. We found that this close relationship with fellow employees was particularly important for many women in their fifties. If they are single, or if their children are gone from home and their old friends often left behind in one or more family relocations, these women look forward to the communal spirit found in friendly and compatible organizations. Their workplaces become centers of social life and interaction.

The same interest in finding community at work is true for many fifty- to sixty-year-old men, as well. For Roberto, the Roman Catholic priest, the role played by his work in providing community is even more poignant. "People," according to Roberto, "have always been the center of my life. My primary ministry has been counseling families, couples, and individuals, as well as preparing and presenting workshops and retreats." The people that Roberto works with are his neighbors, his community, his family. He devotes most of his waking hours to his work and is unhappy when he looks forward to retirement and the loss of this work-based family.

Inherited Expectations

Among the men and women we interviewed were those who were primarily motivated to work by less common factors. Several of the men we interviewed spoke of continuing to meet their parents' expectations. Martin, for instance, continues to practice as a dentist because his father had been successful in the same profession. He took over his father's practice ten years ago when his father retired. He has been a diligent steward of the practice ever since and is proud of helping it grow. Now in his fifties, however, Martin wants a career in which he would be less driven by the money to be made. Like many men who face an "inheritance of expectations," Martin is still struggling with the parental desires that motivated his original career choice. He is beginning to listen to the vocational voices from other rooms that are encouraging him, and other men like him, to begin meeting their own needs rather than those of their parents.

Many of today's women in their fifties inherited a less ambitious set of expectations from their parents. When Carol was in her early twenties, her father told her to go to secretarial school so she could work for a while until she got married. Mary's parents guided her into nursing so she would "always have something to fall back on," in case her inevitable marriage didn't work out. Joan followed in her mother's footsteps and became a teacher. Sally didn't go to work at all; she married her high school sweetheart, who went through college and worked. She made him a home and raised four children. Then, at age forty-two, she sadly found herself divorced, without alimony and without any marketable skills to support herself.

These are familiar stories for the women who grew up in the post–World War II United States. Many of today's women in their fifties inherited a set of "normal" parental expectations that, as women's roles and opportunities changed in the 1970s and 1980s, became increasingly dysfunctional. Many of these women became the reentry adults who helped make college enrollments soar over the past twenty years.

The achieving women of their era who chose to go straight from high school to college and, perhaps, went on to graduate school, either had parents who supported and encouraged their professional and career goals or had the inner strength to forge ahead alone on their exclusive paths, defying both the expectations of their parents and those of the larger society. Today in their fifties, these latter women hold many of the leadership positions in their fields, companies, institutions, and communities. It is these women who blazed the late twentieth-century trails to women's liberation and fuller equality in the world of work. For the most part, there has been little recognition of the heroic efforts these women have made to find new ways to integrate both work and family. Their divorce rates and the stresses they have experienced in the workplace testify to the difficulty of the task. Neither their male partners nor their culture were prepared for them.

For many women in the lower socioeconomic groups, the story is very different. These women inherited expectations that they would both work outside the home and be homemakers throughout their lives. Work, for them, was never expected to be meaningful or fulfilling, only to pay a decent wage and provide good benefits.

Most women now in their fifties — whether they are blue- or pink-collar workers, professionals or homemakers — know that the work their daughters and granddaughters do will probably be very different from the work that they themselves have done. Work options for women have expanded so rapidly and broadly over the past twenty years that even the most highly educated and sophisticated women in their fifties cannot adequately guide their own female offspring when it comes to career planning and job searching. In truth, it is a new day for women and work. Old myths and patterns are now irrelevant.

In spite of all the new work opportunities open to contemporary women, however, the essentials of biology are still with us. As long as women have babies, their time and energies will be divided between their family work, economic work, and community work. This perpetual juggling act is one that men, in their longing to fulfill their roles as fathers, are coming to grips with as well. The ways they handle such juggling will continue to evolve well into the next century.

The release from parental expectations and — especially for women — from social expectations that we are experiencing now in our fifties, thus poses a new challenge about work and a newfound freedom of choice, which is both welcome and stressful.

The Search for Autonomy

Still others we interviewed spoke of the autonomy they want from their work. Some of the women in our study had become disillusioned with the work they were performing for others. They said they were under-paid, under-recognized, and under-promoted, especially if they had entered or reentered the work force in their thirties and forties. Rather than continuing to fight the battles of discrimination, a number of these women have struck out on their own and begun their own businesses.

Women-owned businesses, now the fastest growing segment of our economy, are often small and tend to begin as operations out of the owner's home. Even those women who haven't yet started their own businesses are often motivated in their current jobs by the desire to accumulate enough funds to start their own businesses one day. Glenda, for one, dreams of taking early retirement and opening a small doll shop with her sister. Betty hopes to build on thirty years of experience as a corporate secretary in order to establish her own independent secretarial service. These women are less concerned about financial security in retirement and less interested in the leisure time that retirement offers than are many of the men we interviewed. They are motivated instead by the promise of independence and autonomy.

As we said earlier, for women, their fifties are generally a time when they seek greater independence and autonomy. Even women who are not starting their own businesses ask themselves, "What do I want to be when I grow up?" Although this typically adolescent question may at first appear inappropriate, it is generative and healthy at this time of life also. In many ways, women have had to reinvent themselves many times throughout their lives and may be more experienced and skillful at this task than men typically are. While people who are late in starting jobs outside the home never really catch up on the linear career ladder, the cyclical, ever-changing nature of women's work lives may better prepare them for a lifetime of self-reinvention and self-renewal.

Men in their fifties may also look for increased autonomy in their work, but it is not always easy to find. At age fifty-four, Larry, who had always worked for someone else, decided that if he was ever going to be in business for himself now was the time to do it. The economy had been booming. Franchises were new and relatively easy to get. So Larry, along with his young adult son, opened a franchised retail store. For about five years, the business prospered, but as the economy began to slow down, it became apparent that the store would have to be closed. At fifty-nine, Larry was without work, deeply in debt, and facing his sixties as a depressed, beaten man. Over the last few years, he has taken almost any job in his industry that he could get and his work today has little meaning and minimal autonomy, serving only to provide a steady paycheck.

Increasingly, men have autonomy forced upon them. Dick worked in the same company as a loyal corporate manager for more than twenty years. In a corporate reorganization and downsizing, Dick acquired a new boss who knew little of Dick's achievements and resented his continual references to the past. When an early retirement offer was made to the middle managers, Dick thought it was the best deal he could hope to get, and he retired from the company in his midfifties. "Now what?" he asked himself. And the answers were not there.

Hundreds of managers in Dick's situation are now on the local job market. As a loyal "company man," Dick had risen to a level of responsibility and respect in his job. Now he was left with time on his hands and no significant community or social involvements. His needs to be in the thick of things were totally unmet, and he felt less in charge of his life than ever before. As his options became narrower and his wife became the family's primary breadwinner, Dick decided to move to another city. His previously confident spirit has given way to self-doubt and depression as he tries to start a new job in a new environment.

Larry's and Dick's stories are not uncommon in today's volatile economy. But what happens to a man's sense of self-worth when his primary role—that of worker—disappears? While many men still yearn for autonomy in their work, finding it is not a simple task.

The challenge for both men and women in their fifties, as the clock ticks relentlessly toward their sixties, is to find meaningful and financially beneficial work that can play a central role in their sense of well-being.

The Dilemmas of Work

Men and women in their fifties are just like most adults in our society in often seeing work as a hassle and a source of minor or major stress. Many whom we interviewed spoke about the stress associated with the numerous small but irritating problems and frustrations of daily work—the interminable delays in receiving reports, the incessant bickering among co-workers, and the malicious gossiping that occurs among members of their staffs. It is these petty matters, rather than the big problems, that are often the main sources of stress. This is one area in which fifty-year-old men and women find they have grown less rather than more tolerant. They often cope with these daily irritants by fantasizing about retirement or by daydreaming about and planning upcoming vacations.

Still others we interviewed—especially women—spoke of the ongoing stress associated with making trade-offs between work and other important demands in their lives. In particular, the tasks of juggling, balancing, and integrating work with significant personal relationships are seen as a lifetime challenge. This is the reason why some women have chosen to remain at home to create their work.

Arlene has been struggling for most of her adult life with her identity as a breadwinner (along with her husband) and her roles as a housewife and mother: "If you have a family to handle, too, [work outside the home] is very hard to manage. But it is rewarding when you can earn the money through your own creativity. . . . There are times when I feel inadequate, when we have a hard time financially. We would be more comfortable . . . had I worked [earlier]. My husband said, 'I would rather have you here at home,' and I was glad he felt that way. . . . For many years I did cake baking and decorating, and the cakes were wildly successful. They were enormous fun. Everyone's ego needs that. Mine does." For Arlene, having creative and expressive work—especially when it could be done in her own home—was attractive. Her guilt about leaving her children to go outside the home to work diminished her enthusiasm for getting an outside, but more financially rewarding, job. She also worried about making her husband appear inadequate to the task of supporting a family if she went to work outside the home. No matter what she decided, she experienced stress and conflict. No one choice satisfied all her needs.

We found instances among married couples where one of the partners was ready to retire — or at least back off from an emphasis on work — in order to devote more time to family life, precisely at the time when the other partner was beginning to become successful in a career. Typically, the fifty- to sixty-year-old husband is the one who is burned out in his job and wants to spend more time at home, while his wife is just beginning or in the midst of a successful and professionally engaging career. She wants to spend less time at home precisely at the point when he wants to take more trips, see the grandchildren, or simply spend quiet times in front of the television set.

Rebecca, for instance, who is still actively engaged in her career, is generally upbeat and optimistic about her husband's upcoming retirement, but she is also a bit fearful. She says, "My husband is burned out. He is getting ready to retire next July. That's a goal he is looking forward to. I hope we will be able to handle retirement [as well as we have this working period]. . . . That may be a trying time on the marriage. Maybe you should interview me a year from now! I'm not retiring with him. I feel he can find plenty of things to do and see. I'm not sure whether he will be just retiring from this job or maybe there will be something else he'll want to do on a part-time basis. He's looking forward to it. And I am, too, now."

Mismatched male and female career patterns are likely to increase in future years as more women become seriously invested in their work. We can expect an increase in marital tensions as a result of these incompatible goals in mid and late life. When men and women's work and personal goals conflict even more in their mature years than they did at younger ages, we may see more late-life divorces. However, as women's career paths come to parallel men's more closely, we may eventually find that both men and women, after a full life of dual career and relationship juggling, are ready for a less work-dominated life as they move through their fifties.

For the men and women we interviewed who had made the difficult choice early in life to forgo intimate relationships and children in favor of career, their fifties are often a difficult era. Sam spoke about the trade-off that he thinks is inevitable between a life as an artist and as a parent. He chose, therefore, at a rather early point in his career, not to get married or have children. While he does not regret his decision to become a painter, he does become wistful when talking about his lost opportunity to become a father.

Like Sam, Kathy Ann spoke poignantly about choices she had made between family and career. The prevailing theme of her interview was loneliness. She spoke of the lack of intimacy in her life, her feeling of loss in having "no family and all the things that go with it," and the total lack of options in her life. However, she also spoke proudly of the innovative record-keeping process that she had created over a seven-year period for a local financial firm. "Everyone told me," she said smilingly, "I would never make anything of myself." She was feeling very good about her accomplishment and about herself despite lack of support from members of her family, yet she was fearful about her future and how she would fill the void in her personal life.

Kathy Ann felt that her lack of family was somehow inherent in her decision to commit most of her attention and energy to work. To her, her decision meant that she never had sufficient time or energy left over to meet other people and to learn how to engage them in intimate relationships. Her sense of powerlessness is particularly disturbing. She still has many years left in her life, but she seems to see her early commitments to work as opposed to relationships as lifelong and irreversible.

Claudio, one of the gay men we interviewed, has no significant-other relationship and anticipates that his battle with AIDS can only shorten his remaining years. His commitment to life has engendered a powerful reordering of priorities:

> The time that I have remaining is time to be spent around nature, music, art, working with my hands, developing relationships, but on a sort of—what should I say?—warm plane, not intimate, not highly intimate. I don't feel that I have the energy to develop intimate relationships at this time in my life. I have been hurt in the past. I don't think that I am saying this because I am afraid of being hurt

again. What I am afraid of is losing time. Time
is precious to me. . . . I think that not having married, I may be somewhat spoiled. I see married men
as having a tough life. It shouldn't be so. People
should think about [their lives] after the children
are going to be gone. Even if they don't have children, single people worry about the future, but they
don't think and really plan for the future. They only
worry about the future. They worry about being
sick and they worry about financial security.

Unlike Claudio, who has many interests, Kathy Ann
seems to be caught in a world of stagnation, perceiving opportunities to reinvent herself to be out of her reach. Choices between family and career appear to her to have been cast in stone.
Unfortunately, this same theme appears in the lives of many
of the men and women we interviewed. It is particularly painful when this sense of inevitability and stagnation is found among
couples in long-term relationships. We, the authors, hope that
subsequent generations will be less frequently faced with this
often destructive choice between work on the one hand and love
and friendship on the other.

The real challenge lies not in choosing one over the other
but in finding ways to integrate work and family in a balanced
life-style. Recognition of this challenge is certainly the major
legacy of the women's movement. Over the past twenty years,
both women and men have experimented with new models for
combining family life and work life. Some have succeeded; others
have failed, but as these adults reach their fifties and move into
their sixties, it is important that the lessons they have learned,
regrets and all, be brought into the public arena for debate and
discussion, because the issue of balancing work and family may
be the key to the generativity-stagnation challenge in later life.

New Work Patterns

Work patterns are now evolving that will give both men and
women more flexibility, more autonomy, an adequate economic

base, an opportunity for entrepreneurship, and freedom to organize their family time on their own terms. As we have seen, developments rooted in new attitudes and new technologies promise to transform both the conditions under which individuals work and their motivations for work. As mature men and women, we have as much to gain from these new work patterns as any other age group.

While our fifties decade brings the height of professional prominence and work productivity to many of us, for others of us, our work life presents new problems and challenges. While we have usually moved beyond our parents' expectations by this time, the expectations of our families, colleagues, and social groups create pressures to succeed and to exhibit satisfaction in our work. If circumstances beyond our control intervene, causing unwelcome changes in our work situation, the possibilities for depression and stagnation increase.

It is at this point in life that our motivations for working become especially important. Work that is only a means to financial security or status can become oppressive and onerous. Finding meaning and community in our work can be generative; failing to find meaning leads to stagnation and boredom. Most of us also feel the need to establish a comfortable balance between work and family.

There was a time when one's fifties meant one was nearing the end of one's career and work life. No more. Men and women in their fifties today can reasonably expect to work for twenty or more years, if they wish. Therefore, it is critical that they view their fifties as an opportunity to reinvent their work as a central part of reinventing themselves.

9

Leadership:
Power, Redefinition,
and Self-Renewal

They are able because they think they are able.
— Virgil

Now that we are at the midpoint in our personal century, are we at the pinnacle of our leadership potential? And is this pinnacle truly a position of power? For some fifty- to sixty-year-olds, particularly white males, the answer seems to be a qualified yes. However, a growing number of men and women of all ethnic backgrounds are increasingly making their way into leadership roles. Although the "old boy network" is still alive and well in the United States, in the coming decades we are likely to see its demise.

Positional Leadership and Expert Power

A number of people in their fifties possess *positional power,* which, as its name suggests, comes from occupying senior positions of formal authority. Older men and women often also have *expert power,* which comes from understanding interpersonal relationships or historical perspectives. However, they are less likely to have the kind of expert power that their younger colleagues have gained by keeping abreast of the evermore rapid changes in technology and management procedures taking place in our postmodern society. Thus, it is organizations that do not rely extensively on technology that will be more inclined to value the expertise of men and women in their fifties. Large, old-line bureaucracies and long-standing governmental agencies as well as the more traditional professions, such as psychology or law, which rely heavily on interpersonal relationships, may turn out to be supportive leadership venues for older professionals.

By contrast, high-tech and telecommunications companies that face particularly rapid change and show relatively less concern for interpersonal relationships tend to devalue the kinds of expertise and the historical perspective that older men and women are able to bring. In such companies, the prospect of growing old can be both stressful and frightening, as people try to keep up with accelerating changes, and a growing number of early retirement programs are being instituted, which aim at workers in their forties and fifties. It has become necessary for older workers in formal positions of leadership to join hands with their younger colleagues who hold expert power. This intergenerational cooperation can be a source of self-renewal for men and women in their fifties as competition for leadership between age groups increases.

Yardsticks for Leadership

As we enter our fifties, we typically begin to reflect on our contributions and accomplishments, wondering what we have really done with our lives. Through this reflective process, we develop new yardsticks to judge our achievements and those of others. Because people in major public leadership roles, including our U.S. presidents, probably have about the same amount, or less, of life experience as we do, and because we may have about the same levels of specific skills and knowledge as others who have become more prominent than we have in our fields, three things tend to happen. First, we start wondering about our own success and whether we are as successful as we had hoped to be by age fifty. Second, we become more skeptical of the exaggerated claims made by recognized public and organizational leaders. Are they really as good as they claim to be? Can they really pull off any or all of their programs and promises, given that they are a lot like us in terms of experience, energy, and perhaps even wisdom? Third, at the same time that our skepticism increases, we are also likely to be more compassionate, or at least understanding, about the failures and limitations of our public leaders.

As we identify more closely with those of our own age group who are in leadership positions higher than ours, we may also wonder why we didn't "go for it" and participate more fully in politics, community organizations, or entrepreneurial business activities. Our fifties' assessment and reevaluation causes us to ask, "Have I frittered away my life on small matters and let the big ones go by? What's important in this life, anyway? How can I measure the significance of my efforts?"

Role Models for Women Leaders

A recent study[1] conducted with seventy-seven women in education whose work spanned the years between the 1940s and the mid 1980s revealed two key characteristics among these women leaders: first, collaborative work and management styles, and second, a passion for social justice. Working cooperatively with other women, and some men, who shared their larger vision of social justice, these persistent and talented women leaders transformed the schools, agencies, and institutions of which they were a part. Just as important, their work led other women to follow in their footsteps. Today's women in their fifties have a similar opportunity to pass along the lessons and the motivations they have learned over the past three decades to the baby boomers and those who follow them. In addition, as we learn more about women as leaders, women in their fifties will gain the role models, so rarely found in their earlier years, on which they can base new, effective, and appropriate leadership styles as they grow older.

Leaders as Historians

In our fifties, we are truly walking history books for the first time in our lives. Those of us in our fifties during the 1990s, for instance, are among the decreasing number of people who hold personal memories of World War II, the Korean War, or the Truman and Eisenhower years in the White House. Now, having both these memories and positions of active leadership, we have the opportunity to interpret for those younger than ourselves the lessons to be learned from those years.

Our historical perspective becomes an important tool that we must learn to use to enhance our leadership roles within our own organizations and, if possible, in our public communities. Many of us in our fifties may have been present at the founding of our organizations or at major transition points in their evolution. We are leaders, in part, because we hold this historical perspective, and we often are able to compete with the energy and more up-to-date skills and knowledge of younger men and women simply because we can bring this grounded perspective to problem solving and planning.

The challenge, then, for those of us in our fifties who have become the keepers of institutional memories is to find graceful and effective ways to make the histories of our organizations relevant and useful to others. People who use history only to say, "We tried that before and it didn't work" do not endear themselves to those who are looking for solutions as they manage enterprises in complex environments. So we must avoid being perceived as know-it-alls as we find new leadership roles for ourselves in organizations as participant-mentors.

In these new roles, we in our fifties have opportunities to make history matter by putting our memories and experiences into perspective and extracting those lessons that can be applied to today's problems. The shift of self-image this requires is neither automatic nor simple. Moreover, we must compete in the development of leadership skills and the attainment of leadership positions because there are presently fewer leadership positions than there are leadership candidates. Indeed, in addition to negative motives such as "running away" from larger organizations, one motive for women — and men, also — to start their own businesses is that they can then create positional leadership roles for themselves as business owners and CEOs.

However, in the coming decade, there are likely to be increasing numbers and new kinds of organizational leadership

positions as organizational restructuring spreads more responsibility among more individuals. Those in their fifties who can
offer both historical perspectives on the past and new visions
for the future have the potential to renew both themselves and
their organizations if they take advantage of these new opportunities for leadership.

Leadership for Leadership's Sake

Our interviews suggest that fifty- to sixty-year-old men and
women are less likely to be interested in leadership for leadership's sake than they were when younger. Instead, they are now
much more interested in getting something done that is of value.
We find out what we really care about and then truly care for
it through exerting our leadership. We also tend to support others
who want to get something done—a real sign of maturity and
generativity.

Fifty-year-old men and women also tend to exhibit greater
tolerance and patience than younger people while working with
the complex and often contradictory demands associated with
leadership. One of the major concerns is leadership succession.
This is another aspect of generativity because it is a way of en-
suring that our hard work and accomplishments will live on after
we have gone. We find ourselves asking, "What do I need to teach
the younger men and women in this organization before I leave?"

As age begins to be equated with experience and respect
for experience grows, women vigorously pursue and often are
granted more authority in their fifties than they were earlier in
their lives, often fulfilling a dream from their own early childhood or, perhaps, one handed down by their parents.

Deborah, for example, has helped to establish a community clinic and currently works full-time as the clinic's director
of community services. She also was recently appointed by the
mayor of her city to serve as a city commissioner. Deborah,
who is of Japanese heritage, attributes her human and community service commitment to her parents' and grandparents' values
and actions: "My grandparents and parents were, in their own
way, very community-minded. My grandfather sponsored peo-

ple who came from his village in Japan and was a kind of community spokesperson. He always had money to lend, even during the Depression. He came to Hawaii in 1905 then to [a western U.S. community] to pick oranges. The family stayed in the produce business, and every Sunday, farmers from all around the area would come for support, and we'd have a picnic. My grandma did all the cooking."

In her early life, Deborah focused her energies primarily on raising her children. "Kids aren't with you very long," she says. "You have to take it as it is." As her children grew older, however, she was able to realize her parents' and grandparents' commitments and view her predecessors as role models for community leadership. At the outset, Deborah worked alongside her husband in local politics. Now, she has moved out on her own, becoming particularly interested in leadership among members of the Asian-American community.

Much as fifty- to sixty-year-old women in leadership roles are likely to be perceived as mothers, rather than as potential lovers, male leaders in this age range are also more likely to be viewed in a parental role as fathers, or perhaps even grandfathers, rather than as potential lovers. While this shift in the perceptions of others may not entirely agree with the way fifty-year-olds see themselves, it nevertheless encourages dependence on the older persons in groups, casting them into the leadership roles. In our fifties, others' perceptions cause the warrior-leader role—a role usually taken on by younger men (and some women)—to give way to the paternal-leader role. Older men and women are less likely to be perceived as the visionaries or innovators in a group than they were in earlier years—even if innovating is still their preferred mode. They are now more likely to be viewed as preservers of old practices and traditions in organizations. However, because both men and women in their fifties find they now have a broader repertoire of leadership skills and styles, they are often able to practice situational leadership—shifting styles as the circumstances require—better than younger men and women. They may also become more flexible and tolerant, based on their broader experience and their decreasing investment in "winning."

As we grow older, our goals often become more pragmatic and realistic and less self-serving. We want to make things work, not necessarily always to be right. In a way, we have let go of the trivial for the sake of the overall success of our organizations' fundamental missions. We have become stewards, trustees of our organizations' futures. This is a positive change, both for us and our organizations. It is regrettable, we think, to watch large companies trim or retire their more senior members as part of downsizing just at the time the value of these senior employees is enhanced.

Political and Social Values

Given that people in their fifties tend to be interested in leadership as a means to some larger end, rather than as an end in itself, what are the ends, or values, toward which these maturing men and women strive? Typically, their values reflect both a new traditionalism and a new skepticism. Alex, for instance, found that he began to see "a lot of wasted money in the system, and all of a sudden, restraint seemed like an exciting idea." Alex described himself as having formerly had quite liberal views. Now, he says, "I don't know if it is totally accurate to label myself as conservative, because I still like many [liberal] ideas and programs. I guess I felt a need to get back to the good old traditional values as I became older, and in some sense, I am more conservative than I was."

Many other men and women we interviewed spoke in a similar manner of gaining a new appreciation for "old-fashioned" values: honesty, integrity, and creating congruence between what one says and what one does. Yet, in most instances, this did not mean that they felt a greater reliance on, or even confidence in, the older institutions of our society, such as government, the church, or the press. Instead, there was a growing skepticism about these institutions and a desire to return to what the men and women thought were the fundamental values and simple processes that were prevalent in earlier years.

In our study, the skepticism, and sometimes accompanying cynicism, of fifty- to sixty-year-old men and women took several different forms. Some people have simply given up on established institutions and politicians. Roberto, for example, worked in corporate life for ten years before entering a Catholic seminary and being ordained as a priest in 1970. "Over the years," he noted, "I have become much more liberal. It seems that the major political parties are not really addressing the issues. Especially the plight of the minorities. I am disenchanted with the political leaders that I see today." Yet Roberto hasn't entirely given up on the institutions that politicians lead, feeling that in contemporary times "government action and programs are vitally important to help people to survive and grow." He says that, in contrast, twenty-five years ago when he was a corporate executive he thought "that all people were capable of helping themselves and working toward their own betterment and that government programs were not needed and oftentimes were more of a hindrance than a help."

While Roberto doesn't think that most politicians really care about ordinary citizens, he still believes that government institutions are the only ones that can meet broad social needs. Marsha, a vibrant and active woman and a now divorced mother of three grown children, would disagree with Roberto. She believes that political institutions are not essential. She agrees, however, that most politicians are not worth much. Humans "will survive as a race," she comments, "*despite* the politicians!"

The men and women we interviewed also revealed their growing skepticism and cynicism by retreating from specific party affiliations and shifting to more issue-specific approaches to politics. Gerald, for one, as we saw earlier, has mellowed with age. A graduate of a prestigious law school, he was set in his ways, politically at least, until he began traveling abroad, particularly in Japan. This not only made him more tolerant of other cultures, it also broadened his view of what matters: "Politically, [I've become] really turned off by politicians. I vote person and office and not party. You know, pick the person that has the country's best interests at heart, and that's who I'll vote for, regardless of party affiliation or race or whatever."

Many of the people we interviewed talked about having seemingly contradictory opinions about various political and

social issues. Gerald says he is a conservative on economic issues but a liberal on social matters. Susan speaks about her growing concern about drugs and about law and order. She knows
that this is a conservative stand and, in some way, doesn't seem
to fit with her long-standing commitment to liberalism and the
Democratic Party.

A group of fifty-year-old friends that have met regularly
over the past twenty years used to talk exclusively about liberal
causes. All of them still view themselves as being liberal in the
areas of social justice and disarmament, yet they now spend more
time talking about tax breaks for investments and about new
state and federal programs that offer aid to our ailing economy.
Each believes that his or her economic attitudes are more conservative now, but each also recognizes the complexity of most
issues. Each of them accepts the fact that a self-interested conservative economic view may be inconsistent with a liberal social and political view, even though these views now live side
by side.

Some of our skepticism and cynicism translates into habits
of "thinking globally, acting locally." Benson's earlier liberal
values, for instance, which provided him with energy and a
romanticized vision of an ideal world, are clouded with cynicism. In his work with activist agencies, communes, and religious organizations, Benson feels that he has been "using a
broken lance against the windmill too often." This Don Quix-
ote of the contemporary United States now tends to leave social agencies to operate on their own and channels his energies
into professional work with a focus on changing individuals and
systems through family therapy.

Similarly, Deborah, the Japanese-American activist we
described earlier, finds that her interests in social justice have
tended to become more focused. She now spends more time
working with Asian-American women in her community than
she does crusading for general community causes in which she
believes. She still goes to political rallies in her community. However, she now does so because "most Asian women of my generation wouldn't do these kinds of things"—rather than because

she thinks her participation is likely to be of any major importance in resolving the issues at hand.

Donald is a fifty-eight-year-old recovering alcoholic. He
describes an early political shift in his life and a more recent
personal shift: "Politically, I was brought up as a Republican.
Voted Republican in my first election (for Ike). Never again.
I generally vote for the lesser of the evils. I look for something
between Carlos Castenada and Alan Watts! . . . Socially, I've
mellowed from radical (not thinking about tomorrow), to thinking and preparing for old age. I take care of myself. I jog every
other day, lift weights, and generally stay fit. I was once involved in an [activist organization], but I'm not nearly as involved now."

Mary Anne expressed similar sentiments. She finds that
her concerns are frequently shifting as she assumes different roles
in life. She would like to stay focused on her own world and
her own spirituality as well as her physical well-being. She says,
"I now have less physical energy and so do less for other people. I have more time to think about myself. My values have
changed dramatically — spiritually. What's interesting is that the
way I was a long time ago, when I was growing up, is really
the way I am today. And, in between, a lot of things happened."

Mary Anne now has new family members and grandchildren to think about. Although she describes herself as apoliti-
cal, her new family has given her a concern "about social welfare. [When I didn't] have kids in school, I didn't care what they
did in the school system. Now I have a granddaughter. . . . It
is my problem. . . . It's an issue of responsibility . . . even though
I hate the fact. . . . That's the direction I'll be moving, into being totally responsible, which I guess I'm really not."

For Mary Anne, Donald, Deborah, and many of the other
men and women we interviewed, this mature stage of leadership is both complex and challenging. Just at the point that they
want to shift their attention from broad global issues to concerns of a more immediate, personal nature, the outside world
and a new generation of family members seem to be asking for
their wisdom and experience.

New Opportunities for New Kinds of Leadership

Men and women in their fifties today have grown up and lived
much of their adult lives at a time when both business and community organizations were often modeled on military organizations. They were top-down, hierarchical, linear, and centrally
controlled. Masses of ordinary workers were supervised by a
number of increasingly smaller levels of middle managers who
were supervised by upper executives who, in turn, took their
orders from an elite group of bosses or owners. Careers were
ladders. One had to climb upwards in order to reach the position of leadership, the place where information was tightly held
and from which all resources were allocated.

Today's postmodern organizations are rapidly becoming
flatter, more decentralized, horizontal in their career paths, less
hierarchical, more flexible, and more reliant on information systems that connect dispersed units of work across vast distances.
Personal and rapid response to the customer or client has become a mark of quality. Teams and coordinators who have access to information and can make quick decisions are rapidly
replacing layers of managers and authoritarian bosses who restrict information. Information is power, and information is now
broadly available through databases, computers, and fax ma-
chines, empowering workers at all levels and in all settings.
Brains are replacing muscles as a source of power. The orches-
tration of quasi-independent units of work and political activity
is fast replacing central, authority-based delegation.

As these structural changes occur new opportunities for
new kinds of leadership become apparent. For men and women
in their fifties, this can be a perplexing time. The images of
leadership that they have known in the past become less useful
and less sought after. But new opportunities become available
for those who notice them.

In traditional organizations, only a few could occupy
leadership positions; in the new dispersed network organizations,
many leaders are needed. In traditional organizations, only those
with formal connections could make decisions; in the new, more
fluid and informal organizations, decision making connections

can be made by anyone willing to participate and initiate those connections.

As our organizations change, so do the criteria for leadership change. Diversity becomes an asset as our population becomes more diverse and those on the inside of a particular group have insights into that group's culture that outsiders do not have. Effective leaders will be those who not only can tolerate diversity and manage it, but those who truly value diversity and can access the creativity inherent in various groups.

Those fifty- to sixty-year-old women who have skills that they gained in family life for juggling many projects simultaneously and orchestrating different views can bring these skills into the workplace and the political arena. With these skills, they can build collaborative teams and make the connections that allow network organizations and coalitions to function as integral parts of a coherent yet widely dispersed whole. Leaders sit at the center of these network organizations, not at the top. Women in their fifties are uniquely positioned to assume these kinds of network-organization leadership roles.

Vision is a key characteristic of leadership. Men and women in their fifties are in an excellent position to offer a vision with roots in the lessons of the past. To exert leadership requires energy and deep commitment, or passion, for an idea. There is no better time in life than our fifties for the passionate adherence to an idea to be backed up with the energies that come from reinventing ourselves. We are now still young enough, healthy enough, and mature enough to assert our ideas and to exert our energies in new leadership roles — if we choose to do so.

The great anthropologist Margaret Mead once suggested that meetings regarding the future should always be held with at least one child present in order to remind us who the meeting is for! In our case too, just as we are about to turn perhaps too far inward, the voices of our grandchildren and our organizations and communities draw us back out into the world once again and keep us from becoming exclusively self-serving. In this way, our personal self-renewal and reinvention is often made possible by our new opportunities to reinvent and renew the world around us.

10

Achievement and Failure: Coming to Terms

> Let us, then, be up and doing,
>   With a heart for any fate;
> Still achieving, still pursuing,
>   Learn to labour and to wait.
> —*Henry Wadsworth Longfellow*

A simple sense that we have "made a difference" in at least one organization or business enterprise often becomes important to us in our fifties. However, as we reflect on our achievements, we may also come to sense that the years of greatest productivity have already come and gone. Therefore, the results of our reflection can vary from real self-satisfaction to frustration or even depression.

Alex noticed that he spoke primarily about his past when talking about work. "It sounds like my potential for new successes is limited," he concluded as he evaluated his age, level of energy, and shift of priorities from work to family. The real question for Alex is whether his assessment of his more limited opportunities as a function of age is either accurate or helpful to him in coming to terms with his current life. Others in our study were also assessing the value of their life efforts.

Being Realistic About New Opportunities

We need to be realistic about our capacities and energy levels at this time in our lives. Elizabeth, a fifty-year-old woman who

148

has a master's degree in education, spoke about being "more comfortable because the expectations are given up." Derek, one of her colleagues, who holds a Ph.D. in education, also noted that "there is a midlife transition from going for the brass ring to . . . going for a stable financial state." Going for stable finances is "hard-nosed reality." Both of these professionals represent the healthy development in many mature men and women of giving up unrealistic dreams and expectations about potential achievements. They turn instead to a less glamorous but potentially more productive focus on realistic, achievable ends. Men and women such as Elizabeth, Derek, and Dick (the fifty-one-year-old art and antique dealer from Salt Lake City) have entered a stage in which there is a clearer sense of real-life priorities. According to the person who interviewed Dick, "he wasn't driven or searching as he had been as a young man, nor did he feel that there was anywhere he could go to learn more than he learned by going within or relying on himself and his wife. He felt, in career and marriage, self-contained, self-sufficient, and satisfied."

This realism does not preclude considering new opportunities. Our fifties may hold the potential for even greater accomplishments than in earlier years. Men and women in their fifties speak about this era as a time to harvest the many seeds that they planted during their thirties and forties. They speak about a new sense of self-confidence that propels them into new areas and new challenges. Katherine, a homemaker, proclaims, "I did not have enough self-confidence when I was young and I was intimidated a lot, especially by males." Now that she has had fifty-one years of experience in the world, Katherine has learned that she is capable of doing a lot of things that she didn't think she was capable of doing. "I don't feel as intimidated as I used to because I am more self-confident. I don't care much about what people think of me anymore."

Katherine may be bluffing about her new found self-confidence. Like many of the people we interviewed, she has to deny that she is influenced by others, partially because many of her younger friends and relatives think that she should settle down and come to terms with her diminished capacities, precisely at the point when she has finally found a bit of self-confidence, be it ever so tenuous.

Cynthia is a fifty-one-year-old homemaker and student. She does not want to be limited by the expectations of other people and says, "I know I can do things that lots of others told me were impossible." Even though she graduated from her bachelor's program with a 3.8 (A −) grade point average, Cynthia recalled that an admissions counselor at a major university in her state would not consider her application to a doctoral program because she had six children. Cynthia decided to find another school. She did, enrolling in a nontraditional doctoral program in psychology.

Katherine and Cynthia clearly are not content to play out their fifties as a prelude to retirement. For these two women, this is a sign of health and vitality. Elizabeth, like Derek and Dick, however, is equally healthy in her acceptance of the realities of her life. Less driven than she was earlier in life, she has finally found a new inner peace. Having obtained her master's degree in education, perhaps Elizabeth should have taken the admissions counselor's advice and not attempted to start a doctoral program. Was she still grasping for the elusive "brass ring" that her male colleague, Derek, thinks we ought to outgrow by the time we reach our fifties? Or was she simply revealing the delayed timeline for achievement that is so typical of women who have put off activities of importance to themselves until after their children have grown up?

We admire Evelyn and her determination not to be confined by others' ideas of what "can't be done by someone your age." We like such fifty-one-year-old reachers and dreamers because they reassure all of us, female and male, that options are still open and that we can still reinvent our lives as we choose. Interestingly, because of prior constraints on their dreams, older women may already present new models of renewal for men to emulate. Perhaps there is a gender reversal in some areas of role modeling taking place in our fifties decade.

Keeping Open the Prospect of Growth and Change

If we do not keep open the prospect of growth and change throughout our fifties, then we will be left either with a false sense of contentment or a hollow sense of lost opportunities.

Paul, for instance, who was fired from his managerial position a year and a half ago, is a man who believes he has few opportunities for growth or change. Rather than attempt to reinvent his career, he uses his energies to express a reservoir of anger and frustration regarding what he sees as his limited prospects. He feels betrayed by the company for which he worked for twenty-three years. He felt he had made many sacrifices and had consistently demonstrated his commitment to the organization. His interviewer noted with interest, however, that Paul directed most of his anger at specific individuals within the company rather than at the company itself. He still retains some positive feelings toward the company, and the interviewer, a successful outplacement counselor, concluded that Paul was "devoting a lot of energy and emotion toward trying to reassociate himself with the company. There is an outside chance that he might be able to do some consulting for his former employer, and he is hanging his hopes on this possibility." The interviewer also felt that Paul minimized "his role in the termination and remained preoccupied with the company," and that "in many psychological respects, Paul is still an employee of the company." The interviewer also observed that Paul "doesn't need to work. He is fully vested in his pension and has made some wise investments. It appears that work is more than just a job to Paul. It is a fundamental element of his self-esteem." For Paul, midlife shifts in priorities have not occurred. Early in his career, Paul's sense of self-esteem and work were invested in his job and in his relationship with a single company and they remain that way. At the present time, he is going through a very difficult period.

Given the volatility of the U.S. economy during the 1990s, we can expect many people, particularly men, to be in a similar position. Their identities are embedded deeply in their jobs. They have spent many years building status and security by being diligent workers and now expect to receive rewards in the form of recognition and continuing work. Like Willy Loman in the tragic drama *Death of a Salesman,* many men are simply unwilling, or even unable, to reconcile themselves to their company's, and often their fellow workers', relative indifference to their fate.

When asked what he would do differently in his life if he had it to live over again, Paul said that he would not have tied himself so closely to one company. He wished he hadn't been so naive and trusting. For Paul, losing this long-term job is his greatest failure in life. Yet, he does look with considerable pride toward the achievements of his oldest son, who recently obtained his doctorate in chemistry, and to his success in raising three other children. Paul has come to see his relationships with members of his family as important and has established a closer relationship with his wife and children since losing his job. Yet, as the interviewer noted, Paul continues to hold on both to his identification with his former company and to his fears about being worthless and isolated in his future life.

The Impact of Discrimination

Some men and women that we interviewed—especially those who have experienced discrimination in their lives—spoke about their earlier inability in life to find the right position in which to achieve something of importance. Now that they are in their fifties, they wonder if it is too late to be successful in a career. While many of the men interviewed were somewhat successful earlier in their lives, they now must come to terms with reduced levels of achievement. Many women and ethnic minorities feel that they were never given a real chance. They still hope that success will come.

Eunice, a fifty-two-year-old mother of two grown children, has recently returned to work as a bookkeeper. Her great dream, however, is to be a lawyer: "I like my profession as a bookkeeper; but if I had it to do over again, I would become an attorney. It's too late now."

Susan similarly regrets having failed to pursue a career in law, though she considers her greatest success to be "sticking it out with banking as long as I did [over twenty-two years]. It's a cruel world. . . . I have to take a lot of crap." She wishes that the world had been such in her early twenties that she could have gone to law school and assumed a position in society that she believes would have been less punishing. "I'm satisfied with what I have and what I've got," she reflected. "I'm content, but I would have been much happier as a lawyer." Susan looks forward to early retirement and, like Eunice, expects to travel extensively and spend time with her family.

Like many of the other women we interviewed, both Eunice and Susan believe that they missed being part of women's true liberation. The opportunities for women to enter high-status and high-paying professions came too late for them. They and the other fifty- to sixty-year-old women in our study were young enough during the 1960s and the 1970s to have been influenced by rhetoric about shifting roles and larger opportunities for women. Yet, many of them believe that they are no longer young enough to take advantage of society's shifting perspective. The impact of the woman's movement on their own life choices has been minimal.

However, there were other women we interviewed who had decided in their early forties to obtain advanced degrees and move into new professions. Rita, for example, and some of her more adventurous colleagues grabbed onto the newly emerging career options for women and pursued them vigorously.

Rita was about forty when she went back to school in an Eastern state — preparing to become a minister in her church. Her husband, however, out of work for more than a year, was offered a job on the West Coast, and Rita decided she would "honor her marriage first" and interrupt her religious education in order to move west with her husband. When she arrived on the West Coast, Rita applied to a nearby school and completed her degree in theology. She was ordained in 1985, at age fifty-two, and only regrets that she did not see her potential earlier in life. Rita never felt she had much support from her husband for her work, however, and divorced him soon after accepting a job in a local church.

Rita faced barriers similar to those that Eunice and Susan confronted, yet she was willing to make some difficult choices in order to achieve her own dream. She regrets not having made these choices earlier, yet we must keep in mind that the world was quite different when Rita was thirty years old; becoming a minister was rarely an option for a woman. Caught in the gap between two eras, Eunice, Susan, and Rita were forced to choose between two models concerning how women might best construct their sense of self and lead their lives. Eunice and Susan chose one model — homemaking plus minimal career ambitions. Rita chose the other — fulfilling ambitious career goals relatively late in life. However, both of these models have major costs associated with them and often lead to disrupted relationships and regrets once women reach their fifties. The question, "What if . . . ?" is a haunting one, which appears and reappears throughout many women's fifties.

Similar problems and choices have been faced by many fifty-year-olds who have confronted discrimination because of their race, sexual orientation, ethnic background, or physical disability. Two of the Hispanics that we interviewed spoke of their regrets about having been dissuaded from going to college early in life. They both feel that lacking a college degree has prevented them from achieving financial security and has thwarted their dreams of success in specific professions.

José speaks with great pride of his Hispanic heritage but also says that his lifelong dream of becoming a lawyer was never realized, in large part because of discrimination against Hispanics when he was an undergraduate student during the 1950s. Maria also considers her Hispanic heritage to be central in her identity. However, she also believes that the benefits she associates with this heritage, such as strong family ties and deep concerns for friends and community, outweigh the numerous barriers to career advancement for Hispanics. For both José and Maria, and for other members of ethnic minorities that we interviewed, recent societal changes in attitudes and laws have come too late. Both José and Maria feel that younger Hispanic men and women can now realize their dreams if they are sufficiently motivated and intelligent, but they worry that younger men's and women's career advantages may be counterbalanced by a loss of contact with their heritage and that succeeding generations may find themselves caught between two worlds and two value systems — one Anglo and the other Hispanic — neither being a place that they can truly call home.

Commitment to Others and the Next Generation

Many of the men and women we interviewed revealed a strong sense of generativity, particularly with regard to the lasting contributions they have made. As men and women in their fifties grapple with and try to reconcile issues of generativity versus stagnation, they become involved in expressing a "grand-generativity," which is not rooted primarily in childrearing or other personal cares and responsibilities but in caring for the entire generation that will succeed us in our work and that we are now teaching in our schools.[1] True generativity is rooted in our involvement in the larger society, not merely in our own personal sphere of influence.

Sometimes the person we support emotionally is in a field that we have come to appreciate but in which we are not ourselves very proficient. In other cases, we serve as mentors to younger men and women in our own field and try to help them avoid the problems that befell our own careers. Ned, for instance, is a jazz musician. As an African American, he has suffered the insults of discrimination over many years. Through it all, he has proudly remained a "jazzman." When asked what he would tell people about his life's work, Ned first spoke of being fair and having helped mankind. Slowly, but with growing animation, he became more specific: "I helped other people carry the tradition on to learn music the correct way and the fundamentals." Ned's own musical education helped him see what others needed:

> When I went to grade school in Cincinnati, P.S. 25, they had limited saxophones. It seems to be a problem here in Los Angeles too, limited instruments. . . . At the school I went to, they had few saxophones, and so they doled them out by giving them to the kids with the straight curly hair. Light complexioned. I wasn't dark complexioned. I'm kind of in the middle, but with kinky hair—it was red at the time—and so they gave Dave Young—

[who was to become] the great saxophone player
in Duke Ellington's band—they gave him a sax and
[they gave a sax to] Jimmy, who had curly hair.
Then they gave me a violin. It was a violin that
pulled out of the case from the back. I hated it at
the time.

Ned can laugh now about that violin. He escaped his
schoolmates' insults and his mother's insistence on practicing
by joining the Army. In the Army, he became a talented trum-
peter and sax man; however, the Army also taught him the full
force of racism: "These hillbilly guys from Georgia—the Army
was very racist at the time—got mad because I played late at
night. I drank beer and would practice. I did not play that well
at the time, and they came in and stamped my saxophone flat—
you know, a real expensive horn [that my mother had sent me].
They just flattened it!"

Like José and Maria, Ned is proud of his heritage and believes that the discrimination he inevitably faced led him to become more attuned to the realities and surprising rhythms of life.
He says, perhaps sardonically, that being black in the United
States gives him "a certain muscle. . . . You have to . . . become
really good and fast-footed . . . so I had instant swing. . . . You
have to hurry up and get it, because if you failed, you'd never
get another chance. So you had better be very good, better, really
show out, so that muscle takes great grasp real quick: instant
swing." Ned pops his fingers in a staccato rhythm as he talks.
"In America, it's kind of like the air; it's in the food. If you're
black, you'll know the right way in any situation."

Ned now wants to teach the next generation of black jazzmen the discipline of jazz. He wants to find a way to get them
their own saxophones—regardless of their skin tone or hair tex-
ture. He cares deeply about his craft and about the black experience in the United States, and he finds generativity in his personal commitment to the next generation of jazzmen—even to
those he does not yet personally know. He will flatten no one's
saxophone or personal ambitions.

One of the women in our study, Tricia, similarly finds

generativity and satisfaction in her work with a nonprofit human service agency that is committed to child care for low-income families. She gets paid for forty hours but often works more than one hundred hours per week and loves it. Outside her job, Tricia teaches a theater class and likes to go camping in the wilderness. She worries about not having enough money for retirement and about becoming ill, with insufficient financial resources. She doesn't feel that our society has sufficient respect for women over the age of fifty. Yet, despite her concerns, Tricia concludes that she is leading a rich, satisfying life in which she has ample opportunity to serve other people— many of them strangers. This feeling that satisfaction comes from achievements that reach beyond ourselves is a central ingredient in our generativity in our fifties.

Ella, like Ned and Tricia, cares deeply. She has worked for the past four years with a newsletter that focuses on women's issues among members of her religious community. When asked about her greatest achievements in life, Ella always comes back to her work with this newsletter. This is where she can make a difference.

There are others in their fifties, however, who seem unable to care deeply. They have lost any concern they might have had for other people, especially the younger generation. Sometimes they have also lost their concern for broad societal issues and even their own heritage. They rely on routine and reject the new and different. They seem to shrivel up psychologically, spiritually, and often even physically.

Della is an extreme example of long-term personal stagnation that is still with her in her fifties. Coming from an abusive family, she says she never heard her father or mother laugh nor even raise their voices. She was also battered by her husband over many years.

Della does not think that there is anything important about her; no one will ever "write anything in history" about her. As she speaks, she mentions having raised four children, says that she grew up in a "sort of abnormal life," then decides that the one important thing about herself is that she raised herself after her father's death when she was fourteen. But, she says, she only raised herself "out of total necessity" when she went to live with some "strange people." Thus, even in her major accomplishment — raising herself — Della sees no sense of purpose or forward movement. She has simply survived the onslaughts of a merciless and unfair world.

Another woman, Mary, described a typical day in her life:

> Well, usually . . . I get up, get up with [my husband]. I make breakfast; . . . I make breakfast for David [my son]. . . . David gets himself together. Two days a week I drive [him to school]; the other days I don't drive. When I drive I usually walk later around the lake. Then I do some volunteer work at school on Tuesdays and Monday afternoon. And then I also do some long-term fundraising work, so sometimes I go to meetings for that. I do things around the house — I cook dinner. I don't watch TV; I try to read. Sounds real boring doesn't it? That's how it is. I do the shopping and manage the stuff. Keep the things going.

"Keep the things going." Nothing seems wrong about that, and Mary is active and contributes to her community through volunteer and fundraising activities. These things ought to be generative, but even though Mary laughs when she describes her life as boring, she truly seems to find it boring herself. The key to generativity is not so much our activities themselves as it is our attitude toward the activities. Do they lead to fulfilling our values? Are we caring for those things about which we truly care? Those are the criteria that help us to define the activities that we will find generative.

Perhaps Mary's boredom arises from the traditional roles as cook, chore woman, shopper, and manager of "stuff" in which Mary finds herself. Many women that we interviewed had to break away from traditional homemaker roles to liberate their generativity. Other women, however, have succeeded in finding generativity within their roles as homemakers, spouses, and mothers. They have become active in community affairs and are not apologetic about their involvement.

The Interplay of Generativity and Stagnation

While stagnation alone can rob our fifties of the vitality and new sense of commitment that we should feel and can defeat our opportunity to reinvent ourselves, generativity alone can also make our lives a burden to us instead of a source of deep satisfaction. Generativity must be balanced by some elements that are characteristic of stagnation: continuity, stability, and a sense of history. As Erik Erikson cautions, when we are ceaselessly preoccupied with caring for the larger outer world, we run the risk of wounding our families, relatives, colleagues, friends, and caretakers through neglect or other inconsiderate actions. Yet these people are of immediate importance to us, and our concern for them is likely to be beneficial to us as well as to them. Retaining our concern for those close to us while also reaching out to others is similar to the dual concern for history and for the future that we must have as effective organizational and social leaders. Therefore, we will experience an essential interplay between the forces of generativity and stagnation as we try to develop successful and mature lives in our fifties.

Tina, who works part-time in a hospital as a clerk-typist, spoke with enthusiasm about completing the first chapter of her historical novel about Libby Custer, the wife of General George Armstrong Custer. In addition, Tina has published articles on how to harvest caviar from sturgeon caught in local rivers and has joined a women's writing club, which is publishing a book specifically intended to cheer up nursing home residents. "I've always had this creative streak in me, I guess, but never had a chance to develop it. When I was a child a scout from Republic Studios saw me at my dance school recital and came five times to my parents' home to persuade them to let me go to Hollywood to try out for the movies. I didn't hear about any of this until I was over thirty years old! I was really angry at first for having lost this chance, but I came to understand my parents' protectiveness. Now, at this time, it's the writing urge taking over—I'm getting such wonderful support for it."

The woman who runs the writing club is excited for Tina and has offered editing help for her novel. Such new writing projects are providing generativity and renewal in Tina's life.

In the midst of these abundant interests, Tina struggles to find sufficient time with her family, yet ultimately she finds this time and believes it to be of greatest importance.

A second woman, Pamela, described a typical day in her life in her fifties, showing caring for herself and her autonomy, caring for others, maintaining long-term concerns such as being with her husband, and maintaining continuity in a routine. Smiling with pride and laughing when talking about her husband's cooking, she said,

> I'm up at 5:30 A.M.; shower; twenty to thirty minutes of stretching exercises; activities of daily living; breakfast yogurt with homemade granola, rye crisps, OJ and decaf; read as much of the paper as I can before 7:30 A.M.; drive forty minutes from [my home] to [a nearby urban area] to see clients either at the office or at the long-term care facility for about two hours; do paperwork and phone calls; have lunch; do as much recruiting letter writing as needed in this job as research coordinator; leave 2:30 P.M.; drive back to [my home town], arriving by about 3:00 P.M.; do errands and shopping; home at 5:30 or 6:00 P.M. to fix dinner, except for the days that [my husband] cooks, which means we eat Chinese food or pizza; finish newspaper; check out TV; and finally, in bed by 10:00 P.M.

A former victim of anxiety attacks, Pamela has made the effort to get support, therapy, and counseling in order to move impressively into a period of abundant generativity.

What Makes the Difference?

Why do some men and women stagnate while others regenerate and reinvent themselves? What is the key that makes the difference?

Several different life situations — some of them largely outside the control of the individual person — can lead to stagnation. Inequities in our economic system and patterns of discrimination restrict some people's growth and change during their entire lives, including their fifties. Here, however, we must concentrate on causes of stagnation over which individuals have more control.

First, some people in their fifties find ample opportunity for growth and change but do not experience any pressure to change or grow. They find that safety and security are the only things that they have and the only things that they need or care about. These are the men and women we interviewed who simply wanted to live out the rest of their lives with few demands on them to adjust or compromise.

A second life structure that leads to stagnation is premature success. We peak too soon. The most obvious examples of this are the successful athletes or dancers who reach their peak in their twenties and thirties and must come to terms with the need to shift from the spotlight to a backup role or another career. If they have not made a successful adjustment by the time they reach their fifties, it is usually too late for them to have a successful second career.

For a good many men and women, success came in their forties. They were promoted to a higher position in a corporation, institution, or agency; they scored an artistic triumph; or their children produced enviable school records. They have enjoyed their successes enormously, and their fifties can be anticlimactic as they wonder, "What am I going to do for an encore?"

A very successful insurance executive, for example, whom we shall call Timothy, recently spoke candidly with one of the authors about his concerns as he enters his fifties. He has served as president of a corporation for over ten years and now wants to move on, but to what? "I could accept a position as president of another insurance company," he said dejectedly, "but what difference would that make? I would simply be repeating the steps I already took in making [my current company] more successful."

He is interested in teaching at a nearby college, but doesn't think he would be accepted by the college faculty, given his age and worries that his executive demeanor may intimidate his colleagues on campus. Furthermore, he wonders if he can accept the salary of a college teacher, and feels he would lose status by becoming a teacher. For Timothy, success came, perhaps, too early in life. It is going to be hard to match either the challenge of his current job or the status and tangible rewards he has received over the past ten years. Some difficult decisions lie ahead for this very successful man if he is to remain generative and not stagnate.

A third potential source of stagnation is reliance on either one's own or one's spouse's external signs of achievement. Debra, for example, is a very successful real-estate and insurance agent who has received many tangible rewards for her work, and who says, "Boy! I have won awards in my field. Successes. Yeah. Last year I went to Hong Kong. I earned that trip selling insurance, and I'm well known in the community. I've served in every office in [my fraternal order], and just about every office in [my local community's Republican political organization]." When the interviewer asked her what she had learned from those successes, she replied, "You can get just about everything you want. I mean I wanted that, and I did it."

Debra does laugh as she adds, "That's before I got tired though. . . . I should have listened to my own head instead of someone else. I should have pursued the things I wanted to do and invested [time] the way I wanted to instead of listening to someone else."

However, it appears that she has come to a difficult point in her life. She has begun to hear voices from other rooms in herself that encourage her to establish personal criteria of success. She has lived all her life for external signs of success and is working hard to win another trip to Hong Kong, even though she admits that she doesn't particularly want to go to that city again so soon. Yet winning the trip is a public sign that other people think she is terrific. Inside, however, she doesn't really feel that she is such a terrific person. She is tired and wants to stop awhile to reflect on her real sources of gratification. Time out to reflect may look like the beginning of stagnation, but if it leads to Debra's identifying her real values, it will be a first step toward a generative reunion of her personal aspirations and public goals.

Millie began adjusting her life commitments after a very powerful personal growth experience during the mid 1980s when she took Werner Erhard's est training and learned that she, not someone else, had created the circumstances of her own life. By learning not to control others and by teaching people to take more responsibility for themselves, she was able to transform her marriage and develop a much closer relationship with her elder daughter, whose drug addiction and marriage to a man of another race had created a rift in their relationship.

Millie has spent her life "being a nurse, being professional, being a wife." She had been attracted to work that was praised and supported by people who had become dependent on her — her friends, her patients, and even her own children. Now, she takes these roles "as life, not as myself. The difference is my own inner growth." Later in the interview, Millie said, "[I have] less physical energy and so I do less for other people [and] have more time to think about myself. . . . I am definitely still in a caretaking role, but instead of helping the dependent, I [teach] people to take more responsibility for themselves." Millie learned this lesson from the difficult times she had in raising her own children.

Both Millie and Debra had, in essence, become dependent on external sources of recognition. They needed larger and larger doses of such recognition, ultimately finding little time in their lives for anything else. They had to make an effort to change this pattern.

One of the most common forms of the dependency that can lead to stagnation is reliance on the success of a spouse for one's own sense of achievement and self-worth. Linda, for example, feels that she has been a very successful wife and mother. In assessing her own worth as a human being, however, Linda says, "My husband's personal worth is a reflection of me." She also admits she has always felt unworthy and doesn't know why her husband married her in the first place. She feels fortunate in having found a highly successful man and continues to rely on him for her personal sense of value. In turn, she provides her husband with her unconditional support, something he never received from his parents: "I'm good for my husband's ego and have created a home that is warm and friendly. I'm a good hostess."

Nevertheless, there are hints that, in her fifties, Linda is growing restless. She remarks that her husband would say that he is the strength of the family, but she thinks that she is the strongest, by far. She controls his life in many subtle ways but doesn't want him to become aware of the degree of control that she exerts, seeing herself as the person who remains in the shadows but holds all the strength. Even though she has become more self-assured and autonomous than she was several years ago, she may feel that his awareness of her strength would upset the balance of the marital relationship she tries hard to maintain.

Millie, Debra, and perhaps even Linda believe that there are still many opportunities ahead for growth and personal fulfillment. This belief in new opportunities for growth and development is another key to generativity and to the successful reinvention of self in our fifties. Assessing our achievements and failures, then, becomes a necessary part of our life process. At some point along the path, all of us must evaluate both sides of the tapestry we have woven. For some of us, it may be a painful experience. For other men and women, there will come a real glow of satisfaction. The fifties seem to be that appropriate moment for understanding the real value of our lives — both our failures and our successes. Not all men and women in their fifties are willing to do so. But for those who are, there is still time to make changes, to rekindle hope, and to build new dreams of fulfillment for the decades ahead.

11

Reinventing Our Lives:
The Challenge of Change

Knowledge must be grown in tears.
— Hindu Proverb

As we in our fifties cross into the second halves of our personal centuries, new societal events and trends continue to come along with such rapidity that a full assessment of our future opportunities and challenges is impossible. Still, we can predict the directions of some important changes. The forecasters of our future now talk of the demographic revolution shaping our country as the population as a whole grows older.

In 1988, for instance, two years after the first baby boomers (now estimated to total seventy-five million) began turning forty, thirty-five- to fifty-nine-year-olds started outnumbering the younger group of eighteen- to thirty-four-year-olds for the first time since the 1950s. In 1989, Sean Connery, at fifty-nine, was named by one popular national magazine as the sexiest man alive. As one forecaster noted, age is becoming a badge of honor. Physical beauty in one's fifties is now something to brag about, not conceal. As the 1990s move along, it is predicted that "women everywhere will be more and more inclined to admit to their age, character will count, and character lines — those visible signs of invisible experience — will be seen as an enhancement rather than as a drawback."[1] The aging of the United States, it seems, is less about growing old than about focusing on staying vibrant, fit, and very much alive.

165

However, being told what we should be does not necessarily change our reality. If this perceived shift in social attitudes is meant to give us courage, if it enables us to extricate ourselves from old myths about our fifties, and if it helps us build new, empowering images, then perhaps such descriptions are all to the good. But, as the authors have tried to show, a number of the men and women whom we interviewed, and others like them, believe it it is too late for them to discover new energy in their lives. Can these men and women be motivated toward reinventing themselves through positive predictions and the inspiration of their more generative peers? This remains to be seen.

Generativity in our fifties is directed by a personal, internal, developmental dialogue. If we avoid coming to grips with the redefinitions and search for authenticity that guide true generativity, if we merely choose to become more youthful again, we may have to face this issue in our later years when we have fewer resources to cope with it but when the inner voices we have been avoiding are even more insistent. The challenge is not to regress to former patterns of our youth but to invent new and more appropriate ways to be whole in our maturity.

Our fifties, the authors have come to realize, are about further developing our own humanness — within ourselves, our families, our friendships, our communities, and our organizations. As Warren Bennis says in his discussion of organizational leadership, "We must eternally confront and test our humanness and strive to become more fully human. We operate on a narrow range of the full spectrum of human potential. . . . To be fully human means that we must work hard at coming to terms with unfamiliar aspects of our personalities and it means we have to work equally hard to get other people to widen their responses so that they can understand and accept unfamiliarity and uncertainty. It also means that we must be able to absorb our common humanness without fear of absorption or nothingness."[2] Bennis believes that we in the United States are going through a self-imposed isolation phase. We feel helpless to affect anything beyond our immediate environment, and consequently, some of us retreat into an ever-contracting private world, a retreat which often manifests itself among the affluent as "cocooning" and among the poor as drug addiction. "People float,"

Bennis notes, "but they don't dream. And people without a dream are less easily inspired by a leader's vision."[3] The grief of drug addiction needs no explanation, but cocooning, too, is a form of stagnation.

If we overcome our isolation, our quest for our fuller, common humanness will inexorably lead to an awareness of self that we may never before have known. We will be telling the truth, understanding our strengths and our limitations, testing both our possibilities and our fears about further growth. We will begin an inner journey that will enable us to better understand who we truly are and what we truly care about. We will shuck those familial and social coverings that we may have been wearing on the outside but not owning on the inside, and we will commit ourselves to more meaningful relationships and goals.

Men in Their Fifties

Men between fifty and sixty who, for whatever reasons, have held to the corporate trail throughout their careers often talk of a deadness that they feel inside. On some level, they know that if they cannot connect their work to their inner selves — through using their real talents in their work and finding personal satisfaction in what they do — this feeling of deadness will consume the rest of their working lives. According to Roger Gould, any search for new meaning in our work involves rebalancing five basic motivations. We work to "get bigger" and to deal with a number of possible personal issues. We also work to be able to exercise our full range of talents and capacities, and we work out of necessity. Finally, we work in order to be part of an organization or field that has its own extrinsic meaning.[4]

When men are young, their motivations for working are different from when they are older. At the start of their careers their motives are primarily those of necessity, to get bigger (more invincible), and to be part of something that is, in itself, meaningful. Once men reach their fifties, these reasons are no longer so relevant. It becomes much more important to work in order to confirm their talents and to help them express personal feelings and values that they may have only begun to explore (their voices from other rooms). As they grow older, time becomes too valuable to be spent performing tasks that are meaningless to their authentic selves. For such men, re-inventing their careers in their fifties involves rebalancing and reapportioning Gould's five basic motivations.

Taking a leap of faith into a new career path at this stage of life means facing the unknown — confronting new dangers and new potential and leaving behind their comfortable, safe, and socially sanctioned niches in their former organizations. This challenge may paralyze some men. It may take a critical event — a failed marriage, a serious illness, a death of someone close, a forced early retirement, or a layoff — to force them into the dialogue with themselves that will eventually reveal what they want to do with the rest of their lives.

The search for authenticity is not some overnight magical happening. It often begins in men's forties and stretches across the entire decade of their fifties. Gould states that during this time, "work loses its illusory magical protective powers and [as we men in our fifties become] more in tune with our instincts and impulses, we become authentic adults, true to our innermost selves. We generate our own interests, motivation and values. Because we have decided which things really have meaning for us, we see clearly just how we want to spend our time. We no longer fear bosses or idealize and imitate mentors. We stop being false protectors to women and require instead a relationship of two independent adults." Becoming authentic is exactly what our fifties are all about. We no longer need to play games and can be real to ourselves and to others. As we become more authentic with ourselves and demand higher levels of authenticity from others, we "automatically become generative: we provide a model of a real person rather than a collection of roles. Our children and our juniors learn more about life from us."[5]

In early 1989, a study of more than four thousand male business executives at the middle and senior levels of management revealed widespread dissatisfaction.[6] Forty-eight percent of all the middle managers surveyed expressed great frustration. Their lives seemed empty and meaningless. Of the senior executives, 68 percent felt they had neglected their family lives to pursue professional goals; half said that if they could start over again they would spend less time working and more time with their wives and children. Such astonishingly negative responses provide a sad commentary about the impoverishment that characterizes executives who hug the corporate ladder throughout their careers. It is even sadder to realize that such issues are neither understood nor heeded within these organizations.

A man's search for inner growth is not yet something with which most of our society's organizations are comfortable. Most organizations do not encourage the time-consuming reflection and self-questioning that could give more meaning to people's lives and avoid the frustration the managers and executives in the study said they experienced. On the contrary, such a journey is frequently viewed as a self-indulgence that neither enhances an employee's value to the company nor adds to the bottom line.

Only recently have sabbatical leaves to explore reenergizing career paths been considered viable rewards for long-term, loyal employees. Such sabbatical policies are likely to become more popular in the decades ahead, as business leaders come to value the fuller development of their employees. Periods of refreshment or time for family caregiving are likely to be more commonly available to many workers. Such opportunities for reexamination will enable men to spend time reaching for that core of internal truth and coming to grips with the necessary career choices of their fifties decade. Taking this kind of time-out for reflection and other personal activities does not necessarily mean that men must opt for entirely new careers. Rather, they can reassess their careers in the light of their emerging values, which may soon include a need for more community and more creativity. In the long run, they, their companies, and those closest to them will benefit.

Women in Their Fifties

For women who have been primarily homemakers, the road to authenticity in their fifties often leads outside the home. However, many women, both homemakers and those who work outside the home, feel a need for a new kind of self-fulfillment and, perhaps also, more autonomy and more leadership roles. Some women seek these new opportunities for growth within the community. Others enter, or reenter, the business world—a number of them with entrepreneurial efforts of their own. Still others emerge in the political arena, particularly at local and state levels—areas in which women's progress is becoming more and more evident.

Since political leadership is still strongly linked to corporate leadership, economics play, even locally, a crucial role in women's opportunities at this age. Although there have been dramatic changes in the corporate marketplace, women still have a long way to go to achieve economic and political parity with men.

In the 1970s and 1980s, women entered many professions at a breathtaking pace. In schools of law, medicine, business, architecture, and journalism, women now make up some 40 percent of the students and are a growing number even in the male-dominated schools of engineering. From 1960 to 1979, median earnings of those women working full-time were comparatively stable—approximately 59 percent of the earnings of men, a gender gap of 41 percent. But in 1990, the gap began a steady fall, dropping below an estimated 30 percent.[7] Despite these encouraging signs, women are still not much in evidence in the real power roles. Only 2 percent of the chief executive officers of major corporations are women and fewer than 10 percent of all directors on all corporate boards, while on most public and community boards and commissions, women are either minority members or a mere token presence.

While many men in their fifties realistically view the attainment of leadership roles as both a possibility and an important foundation for generativity, women in their fifties today, by and large, do not yet see themselves—nor are they perceived by others—as potential leaders outside the home. Although, women are finally making serious advances in their professions and career roles, resistance to rallying behind woman leaders is still very strong.

However, some new arenas for leadership are now emerging. First, across the country in every state, small groups of women, predominately in their fifties or older, have begun to form organizations of their own which identify, celebrate, and nurture women's leadership. While these organizations hold enormous promise for younger women, primarily in their thirties and forties, to acquire role models, skills, and relationships with slightly older and more accomplished women, this growing organizational base can measurably increase both the numbers and competencies of women as leaders, even in the next few years. As older women begin to share more explicitly with younger women what they have learned about the requirements and strategies of effective public leadership, the current gender-based leadership gap may close further.

The second route to leadership is through women's careers and professions. The "glass ceiling" remains a serious barrier to women's achievement in the corporate world, but the shift toward the values held by the baby boomers of equity between genders and ethnic groups will crack the glass ceiling and allow more women to rise into leadership positions.

There is a third alternative route to leadership for women. It is similar to the traditional female leadership roles in the private arenas of family, home, and neighborhood. Women's influence on others have always been especially profound in their nurturing of the next generation. This role will not change— even though men will increasingly share these personal leadership opportunities as they begin to take more seriously their own caretaking and nurturing roles.

Women who are now in their fifties have an enormous opportunity to lay the groundwork of their own generativity by conceptualizing and transmitting what they have learned to younger women. At home, in the neighborhood, in organizations, in the workplace, and in public office, women are reaching out to other women, not only as sources of psychological support but also as mentors and colleagues. Over the next decade, we should begin to see some important shifts. Instead of competing with each other for the rare leadership positions open to them, women will begin helping each other to assume multiple positions of influence in all arenas of U.S. life. Instead of adopting male competitive attitudes, and becoming "more male"

than their male colleagues, women will become more collaborative and will imbue public life with their nurturing values of
caring, sensitivity, and continuity. To reinvent oneself in these
ways in one's fifties is an act not only of personal value but also
of social value.

Men and Women Together

As collaboration among women and between men and women
becomes more common, mutually generative efforts will begin
to provide innovative renewal and reinvention strategies. Our
fifties and the years that follow will become less invisible and
more dynamic. Perceptions of aging will give way to images
of blossoming and invigoration. Leadership roles in various
aspects of our lives will replace early retirement roles. Both men
and women will aspire to new levels and new ways to renew
both themselves and their communities.

    None of us will be successful, however, if we fail to use
our fifties to understand truly who we are. We shall never sort
out our most nourishing and fulfilling roles unless we move into
that deeper level within ourselves in search of our own authenticity. This does not mean that we will completely avoid disappointments and reversals. Yet, for those of us who have connected to our true values and goals, facing our failures as well
as our achievements, and continuing to participate in a world
that may bounce us around on occasion, is generative. It cannot stop our caring about what matters to us, because, now,
our sense of meaning resides within us. It is not the meaning
imposed by the external social, cultural, or business world that
dominated our earlier decades of growth.

    Men and women who achieve this kind of self-integration
in their fifties are the giants among us. But even those among
us who feel that our lives are meaningless can stop that feeling
from consuming us if we are willing to discover and pursue our
sources of true meaning. We can reinvent ourselves, and in that
reinvention we can come fully alive again.

12

To the Next Generation:
Preparing for Your Fifties

Such is life —
Seven times down,
Eight times up!
— *Japanese Proverb*

The voices of the many men and women we have listened to in preparing this book and our own experiences in living through our fifties suggest that there are four major messages for men and women who are now in their forties that will help them make the most of their fifties.

MESSAGE ONE
Be Ready for Challenges
and High Levels of Activity

When those of us who are now in our fifties were in our own forties — and certainly many of the baby boomers that the authors have talked to agree — we anticipated that our fifties would be a period of consolidation, reflection, and leisure after our years of trying to achieve success in our careers, building relationships, raising children, engaging actively in sports, and participating in community events.

But instead of being a slower decade for most of the fifty- to sixty-year-old men and women we interviewed, their fifties have been either the busiest or among the busiest decades of their lives. In our fifties we are often in demand for our expertise, our accumulated wisdom, or our informal or formal power. It is during these years that much of what we have worked for all our adult lives comes to fruition.

Our fifties often represent the height of our careers: We are the busiest and the most productive we have ever been, and often at the peak of our earning power. Now that our children are grown, we are willing to expend more time and energy on our own work and major goals. We've lost parents, become grandparents, and nurtured spouses, friends, and lovers through life-threatening or life-ending diseases. Even our inevitable encounters with mortality in this decade have provided fuel for an incredibly uplifting and powerful period of growth.

Many women who are making up for lost time, mostly due to the years spent childrearing, develop high career expectations in their fifties, making this decade particularly hectic. It's a do-or-die time, a hurry-up-it's-late time. The difficulties faced by older women who want to reenter the workplace after years of absence, or return to school to hone old skills, catch up with new technologies, or change career directions also demand a high level of effort.

We want our younger colleagues to be aware that a mismatch often occurs in this period of life between men and women who have been together over the years. While men are often contemplating retirement and slowing down at work, women are often gearing up. Men's and women's opposing patterns strain marriages and primary relationships. He wants to travel and play golf while she is preoccupied with issues at work and is striving for a promotion. Schedules clash. Priorities diverge. While she looks outward, he turns inward. These incompatible rhythms in men's and women's work lives are likely to become more disruptive.

Restructuring in the U.S. workplace is now displacing many middle managers. The jobs to which women now in their fifties have long aspired are fast disappearing from the organization chart. Having the glass ceiling vanish because the positions beyond have vanished is not what women expected to happen. There seems to be no "up" on the career ladder anymore. Where, then, should one go? What does one aspire to do?

For the men who once held those vanishing middle management positions, the dilemma may be even more severe. The job market is not kind to older men, either. In many American corporations, "early retirement" is fast becoming a euphemism for "layoff." While one's job may be ending, one's career is not. "It's too early for fishing trips and golf every day," many men are saying to themselves and to each other.

Enter the phenomenon of entrepreneurship. Former managers, both men and women, are starting their own businesses, developing consulting firms, and buying franchises at rates never before imagined. This is happening in the decade of our fifties, the "invisible decade," more than at any other time in our lives. Not only are the technological revolution, the information age, and the global economy rendering many mature people's skills obsolete, but the idea of being an object of unpredictable corporate decisions is becoming less and less appealing, especially to creative and energetic people.

For those now in their forties, their next decade promises more of the same. A new style of work life that is essentially generative is beginning to redefine the U.S. labor force, as men and women in their fifties set out on their own, in unprecedented numbers, to start up new businesses and professional activities. Nothing in our experience, tradition, or schooling has prepared us for these changes. But they are unmistakable and real.

Among the most interesting aspects of this generative workplace revolution are the partnerships being formed by people with complementary skills, who may be a decade or more apart in age. Former mentors and pupils are becoming colleagues in new ventures, balancing mature experience with young energy and complementing political savvy with technical skills. These alliances are promising and creative and bode well both for the U.S. economy and for the individuals involved. There are few signposts or maps to follow, however, as is true in all revolutions, and there will be many false starts and broken hearts, to say nothing of depleted bank accounts. Our fifties are indeed a time of risk taking.

There are three ways people can prepare for this period of challenge and activity.

Be Ready to Make Difficult Choices
Among Competing Priorities

In our fifties, many of the seeds planted earlier in our lives are beginning to sprout. Which ones are still important? Which are only
important because we have already spent so much time on them or
made so many sacrifices to plant and water them that we can't
bear to abandon them? We need somehow to ignore our sunk
costs and concentrate instead on those projects that still hold our
attention and are worthy of our continued allegiance.

One's forties is not too early to begin sorting out priorities. This includes separating out those values that linger on,
unexamined, from decade to decade. Do we really need that
big house that we dreamed about when we were in our twenties? Do we really need to spend so much time perfecting our
golf game? Is it now time to set aside our childhood dreams of
marrying Prince Charming and having three perfect kids? Can
we lead a fulfilling life without a spouse or children? These are
the kinds of difficult questions to address during one's forties,
even though the answers may not finally come until one's fifties.

Remain Open to Change

We can't simply go on doing what we have always done while
adding on a few more projects, a few more responsibilities, or
a few more values. The key developmental stages that we move
through in our adult lives do not simply call for new skills, activities, or relationships to be added to the existing core, as was
the case when we were children. Rather, each new life stage
calls for the substitution of new skills, activities, and relationships for those old ones that are no longer important. As we
substitute the new for the old, we also deepen our commitments.
Quality typically replaces quantity; depth replaces breadth.

As we abandon aspects of our old selves that provided
us with many past successes and that are still sources of comfort to us, we must also anticipate feelings of grief. We are shed-
ding the old skin and growing a new one. This is painful but
essential in the reinvention of self.

Be Open to New Roles and Responsibilities

When new seeds begin to germinate, men and women in their fifties often feel drawn to nurture and sustain new projects or ideas. We no longer are interested only in generating ideas; we also want to see them carried out.

However, as we realize that we may not be willing or able to complete these tasks all by ourselves, we begin to look for dependable younger persons to carry them forward. We assume the roles of teachers or mentors — encouragers and supporters of others. This shift requires an attitude of stewardship and caring and often evolves into new leadership roles and responsibilities within a family, an organization, or a community. As we learn to share the spotlight with others, our touch is lighter, our attitudes more mellow, and we gain a new spirit of generosity.

MESSAGE TWO
Enter Your Fifties with Sufficient Support

In order to successfully address the challenges and activities of our fifties, it is essential that we have supportive, nurturing relationships with our spouses or lovers, families (however constituted), and significant friends. The fifties is not a comfortable decade in which to be alone. Those in their late forties will want to ensure that the people they care about are around when they most need their support. One's forties are the time to establish or improve the significant relationships in one's life.

The main issue is: Will you culminate your primary relationship in one form and recreate that relationship in a more appropriate form, remaining committed to the same person? Or, will you terminate your marriage or relationship and regenerate the primary relationship in your life with a new person? In either case, whether to live alone or with someone else is at the heart of the issue.

In our fifties, as our parents' generation begins to pass away, we become the keepers of our families' histories. In our fifties, we become family leaders and our responsibilities deepen. But even as we become the leaders in our families, we also begin to rely on other members, especially our adult children, for their support. As we move into our fifties, our grown-up children help us to keep in touch with what is going on with the next generation and may surprise us by turning out to be among our best friends when we face a crisis or dilemma in our own lives.

One's forties is also an excellent time to renew old friendships that hold new seeds of growth, to firm up collegial ties, and to develop new relationships that provide intimacy and acceptance. During their fifties, both men and women tend to focus on fewer relationships that are of greater importance. This is appropriate, yet this focusing opens up a risk of isolation. We still need to keep in touch with other people while backing away from other concerns during our late forties, in order to retain a basis of support for changes that are likely to be made in our early fifties.

By our fifties, we have come to be less judgmental and we have learned to accept those we truly care about on their own terms, "warts and all." Our fifties are a time when we dig deeper in those relationships and put new energy into the ones we truly hold dear.

During our fifties, in addition to partners, family members, and friends, another source of support may be assistance from professionals, whether this be pastoral counseling, psychotherapy, or career planning. Seeking competent sources of this support is best done prior to one's fifties, before the garden springing from the new seeds begins to grow rapidly and the gardener begins to feel overwhelmed.

Support can also come in the form of maintaining and improving one's physical health. One's forties are the years in which to begin regular medical checkups, embark on an appropriate nutritional and exercise program, and build a solid base of physical vitality in preparation for the demands of one's fifties. Physical health—as well as psychological and spiritual health—can be further enhanced by the search for sanctuaries that provide a time and place, apart from daily activities and demands, to reflect on and nurture one's own inner life.

MESSAGE THREE
Act on Your Growing Interest in Generative Activities

The men and women interviewed for the authors' study told us many wonderful stories about their growing interest in teaching and mentoring younger men and women. They told us about satisfactions gained not only from their own accomplishments but also from the accomplishments of younger men and women whom they had trained, supported, and advised. Forty-year-olds might begin working on their own generativity by acting on their newly emerging interests in teaching, mentoring, and counseling others. Perhaps volunteering for a Big Brother or Big Sister program or teaching a course at a local community college makes some sense. On a daily basis, one can be a role model or a source of inspiration for others by moving into a position in one's organization or community that allows for more direct contact with younger subordinates in a training, teaching, or supervisory role.

A second way in which generativity is found and expressed by fifty-year-olds is by being creative — in storytelling, writing, painting, and so forth. When people enter their fifties, they often want to produce something that will endure and in which they can take pride. One's late forties is a good time to begin exploring differing ways in which this enduring productivity might take place.

People are also generative during their fifties through public service. It seems to be increasingly important to many fifty- to sixty-year-old men and women to serve other people in their communities in a tangible manner: for example, in hospice, habitat, and crisis hotline programs. Baby boomers might wish to anticipate the emergence of interests in these areas and begin shifting their attention from traditional leadership roles, such as fundraising or board membership in community service organizations, to roles as direct providers of services. In our fifties, we often want our volunteer efforts to be more direct and personal. One's forties are the time to begin this exploration.

Once again, generativity means caring deeply for that

which we most care about. It means identifying something truly important to us and acting in a consistent and sustained manner to ensure that it is properly cared for. We must identify that which is of "ultimate concern"[1] to us and then act upon that concern.

Generativity involves an honoring of and interdependence with other people. While diversities among us — life-styles, cultures, ethnicities, national backgrounds, ages, values, gender — must be respected, our world's need for collaboration and teamwork is also increasing. Because so many major forces are now converging on the gateway to the twenty-first century, we have an unprecedented need for competent and visionary community leadership in the area of collaborative diversity, leadership that recognizes that people of various ages and cultures see things from different perspectives, hold different values.

The key message that the authors wish to impart to those in their forties about generativity is: Learn how to gracefully terminate that which is ending and is no longer functional and learn how to generate that which is beginning and can define a new future.

MESSAGE FOUR
Replace Current Dominant
Concerns with Emerging Concerns

Our fifties is a decade in which our interests and needs are likely to shift and become more diverse. In our forties, we may be preoccupied with work, yet find that in our fifties family is of growing importance. Or we may discover that a dominant concern with family in our forties has given way to an emerging interest in career or public service in our fifties.

This message to the baby boomers is about cultivating a willingness to accept change and an openness to explore one's own deeply rooted priorities, values, and concerns. Typically, the shifts that do occur in our fifties do not reflect deep changes in our core values. Instead, they reflect our growing impatience with acting out values and activities that were never at the core of our own lives but were imposed by our parents, organizations, community, and society. Our fifties is the critical decade for disengaging from these false values, turning to our true values, and acting consistently with these true values.

Moreover, the authors have learned from many of the men and women we interviewed that in our fifties a spiritual life often emerges or reemerges, owing to our midlife efforts to reintegrate all those elements from our childhoods and our early adulthoods that had become fragmented or that were inconsistently developed. It is usually not a spirituality that makes non-churchgoers into churchgoers. Instead, it is a redefining of our moral and ethical positions and responsibilities.

Conclusion

As we move through this once invisible decade of our fifties, we try to rebalance our lives. We test new definitions of what is normal in our life-styles. We seek new ways to be married, to be single, to be in intimate relationships, and to be together in groups and families. We discover new ways to be with our children, our grandchildren, and our friends. We begin to view former competitors as potential colleagues. Our students or younger colleagues become our partners. We focus our interests. We seek purpose, not merely position. We search for integrity and are no longer willing to accept triviality.

Each of us is looking for good people in good organizations with whom to do good work. We are in what may prove to be the most productive period of our lives, and we are employing our new energy thoughtfully. We are simplifying, not making more complex. Choosing, not being chosen. Giving, not expecting rewards. Digging deeper, not widening or spreading too thin. Discarding, not accumulating. Speaking, not remaining silent. Listening, not ignoring. Giving ourselves permission to live and do as we see fit, not as others define what is right for us. Reexamining. Redefining. Renewing. Reinventing.

To the baby boomers, now in their forties, the authors wish to say, Welcome to your fifties! This decade, in all its many dimensions, promises to be the richest and the most satisfying time of your life.

Research Questions

The following questions were asked to elicit the personal stories of the seventy-three men and women in their fifties who were interviewed (in California and elsewhere) for this book by graduate students from the Professional School of Psychology. The interviews lasted from one to three hours each and took place between 1987 and 1989.

1. What do you feel is important for me to know about you?
2. Imagine that you have been given an award for some aspect of your life. What does this award say?
3. What do you feel have been your greatest successes and failures up to this point in your life? What have you learned from them?
4. Do you have a spouse or significant other? Age? How would you describe your relationship with this person? Have there been significant changes in the nature of your relationship to this person?
5. Do you have children? How many? Ages? How would you describe your current relationship with your children? Have there been significant changes in the nature of your relationship with your children? Can you describe these changes?

6. Are you a grandparent? If so, what is your relationship to your grandchildren?

7. Do you have other important people in your life? Who are they? How would you describe your current relationship with this person [these people]? Have there been significant changes in the nature of your relationship with these people? Can you describe these changes?

8. How have your own values changed, if at all, politically, spiritually, and socially?

9. I would like you to describe three days in your life during the past year. First, I would like you to describe a very special day, a "red-letter" day during the past year. What made this day special? Second, I would like you to describe a lousy day during the past year. What made this day so bad for you? Finally, I would like you to describe a typical day during the past year.

10. If you could do it all over again, what would you keep and what would you change in your life?

RECOMMENDED
READINGS

Astin, H. S., and Leland, C. *Women of Influence, Women of Vision: A Cross-Generational Study of Leaders and Social Change*. San Francisco: Jossey-Bass, 1991.

Belenky, M. F., Clinchy, B. M., Goldberger, N. R., and Tarule, J. M. *Women's Ways of Knowing: The Development of Self, Voice, and Mind*. New York: Basic Books, 1986.

Bellah, R. N., Madsen, R., Sullivan, W. M., Swidler, A., and Tipton, S. M. *Habits of the Heart: Individualism and Commitment in American Life*. Berkeley: University of California Press, 1985.

Bennis, W. *Why Leaders Can't Lead: The Unconscious Conspiracy Continues*. San Francisco: Jossey-Bass, 1989.

Bennis, W., and Slater, P. E. *The Temporary Society*. New York: HarperCollins, 1968.

Bergquist, W. *The Postmodern Organization*. San Francisco: Jossey-Bass, forthcoming.

Blaker, K. *Celebrating Fifty: Women Share Their Experiences, Challenges, and Insights on Becoming 50*. Chicago: Contemporary Books, 1990.

Bly, R. *Iron John: A Book About Men*. Reading, Mass.: Addison-Wesley, 1990.

Boulding, E. *The Underside of History: A View of Women Through Time*. Boulder, Colo.: Westview Press, 1976.

Chodorow, N. "Family Structure and Feminine Personality." In M. Z. Rosaldo and L. Lamphere (eds.), *Woman, Culture and Society.* Stanford, Calif.: Stanford University Press, 1974.

Dowling, C. *The Cinderella Complex: Women's Hidden Fear of Independence.* New York: Pocket Books, 1981.

Ehrenreich, B. *The Hearts of Men: American Dreams and the Flight from Commitment.* New York: Doubleday, 1983.

Erikson, E. H. *The Life Cycle Completed: A Review.* New York: Norton, 1985.

Erikson, E. H., Erikson, J. M., and Kivnick, H. Q. *Vital Involvement in Old Age.* New York: Norton, 1986.

Friedan, B. *The Feminine Mystique.* New York: Dell, 1963.

Gilligan, C. *In a Different Voice: Psychological Theory and Women's Development.* Cambridge, Mass.: Harvard University Press, 1982.

Gould, R. L. *Transformations: Growth and Change in Adult Life.* New York: Simon & Schuster, 1978.

Greenberg, E. M. *Weaving: The Fabric of a Woman's Life.* Littleton, Colo.: EMG and Associates, 1991.

Hardesty, S., and Jacobs, N. *Success and Betrayal: The Crisis of Women in Corporate America.* New York: Franklin Watts, 1986.

Howells, J. G. (ed.). *Modern Perspectives in the Psychiatry of Middle Age.* New York: Brunner/Mazel, 1981.

Johnson, R. A. *He: Understanding Masculine Psychology.* New York: HarperCollins, 1974.

Johnson, R. A. *She: Understanding Feminine Psychology.* New York: HarperCollins, 1976.

Jung, C. G., *Aspects of the Masculine,* ed. J. Beebe. Princeton, N.J.: Princeton University Press, 1989.

Kanter, R. M. *Men and Women of the Corporation.* New York: Basic Books, 1977.

Kean, S. *Fire in the Belly.* New York: Bantam Books, 1991.

Klein, E., and Erickson, D. (eds.). *About Men: Reflections on the Male Experience.* New York: Pocket Books, 1987.

Levinson, D. J., with Darrow, C. N., Klein, E. B., Levinson, M. H., and McKee, B. *The Seasons of a Man's Life.* New York: Ballantine, 1978.

Lowenthal, M. F., Thurnher, M., and Chiriboga, D. *The Four Stages of Life.* San Francisco: Jossey-Bass, 1975.

McGill, M. E. *The 40- to 60-Year-Old Male: A Guide for Men —
and the Women in Their Lives — to See Them Through the Crises of
the Male Middle Years.* New York: Simon & Schuster, 1980.

Miller, J. B. *Towards a New Psychology of Women.* Boston: Beacon Press, 1976.

Neugarten, B. L. "Continuities and Discontinuities of Psychological Issues into Adult Life." *Human Development,* 1969, *12,*
121–130.

Norman, W. H., and Scaramella, T. J. (eds.). *Mid-Life: Developmental and Clinical Issues.* New York: Brunner/Mazel,
1980.

Popcorn, F. "Down-Aging." *Lear's,* September 1991, p. 130.

Rubin, L. *Worlds of Pain.* New York: Basic Books, 1976.

Sheehy, G. *Passages: Predictable Crises of Adult Life.* New York:
Bantam Books, 1977.

Sheehy, G. *Pathfinders.* New York: Bantam Books, 1981.

Sheehy, G. *The Silent Passage: Menopause.* New York: Random
House, 1991.

Smelser, N. J., and Erikson, E. H. (eds.). *Themes of Work and
Love in Adulthood.* Cambridge, Mass.: Harvard University
Press, 1980.

Vaillant, G. E. *Adaptation to Life.* Boston: Little, Brown, 1977.

Viorst, J. *Forever Fifty and Other Negotiations.* New York: Simon
& Schuster, 1989.

Williams, R. H., and Wirths, C. G. *Lives Through the Years.* New
York: Atherton Press, 1965.

NOTES

Chapter One

1. For example, C. Gilligan, *In a Different Voice: Psychological Theory and Women's Development* (Cambridge, Mass.: Harvard University Press, 1982); and M. F. Belenky, B. M. Clinchy, N. R. Goldberger, and J. M. Tarule, *Women's Ways of Knowing: The Development of Self, Voice, and Mind* (New York: Basic Books, 1986).
2. See R. Bly, *Iron John: A Book About Men* (Reading, Mass.: Addison-Wesley, 1990); and S. Kean, *Fire in the Belly* (New York: Bantam Books, 1991).
3. D. J. Levinson with C. N. Darrow, E. B. Klein, M. H. Levinson, and B. McKee, *The Seasons of a Man's Life* (New York: Ballantine, 1978).
4. L. Rubin, *Worlds of Pain* (New York: Basic Books, 1976).
5. E. H. Erikson, J. M. Erikson, H. Q. Kivnick, *Vital Involvement in Old Age* (New York: Norton, 1986), 37.
6. Erikson, Erikson, and Kivnick, *Vital Involvement in Old Age,* 44–45.
7. These voices are the theme of T. Capote's early book *Other Voices, Other Rooms* (New York: Random House, 1968).

Chapter Two

1. Erikson, Erikson, and Kivnick, *Vital Involvement in Old Age*.
2. R. L. Gould, *Transformations: Growth and Change in Adult Life* (New York: Simon & Schuster, 1978), 41–42.
3. Erikson, Erikson, and Kivnick, *Vital Involvement in Old Age*.
4. B. L. Neugarten, "Continuities and Discontinuities of Psychological Issues into Adult Life," *Human Development*, 1969, *12*, 121–130.
5. Erikson, Erikson, and Kivnick, *Vital Involvement in Old Age*.
6. Levinson and others, *The Seasons of a Man's Life*.
7. Gilligan, *In a Different Voice*.
8. J. B. Miller, *Towards a New Psychology of Women* (Boston: Beacon Press, 1976), 83.
9. Gilligan, *In a Different Voice*, 170–171.
10. E. M. Greenberg, *Weaving: The Fabric of a Woman's Life* (Littleton, Colo.: EMG and Associates, 1991), 87–89.
11. Levinson and others, *The Seasons of a Man's Life*. As before, Levinson and his colleagues ascribe to forty-year-old-men's behavior what we believe is now more typical of fifty-year-olds.
12. Gilligan, *In a Different Voice*.

Chapter Three

1. Statement made by R. Shukraft, Th.D., an adjunct faculty member at the Professional School of Psychology, San Francisco, California.
2. Belenky and others, *Women's Ways of Knowing*.
3. C. G. Jung, *Aspects of the Masculine*, ed. J. Beebe (Princeton, N.J.: Princeton University Press, 1989).
4. R. A. Johnson, *He: Understanding Masculine Psychology*. (New York: HarperCollins, 1974), 5.
5. V. Woolf, *A Room of One's Own* (Orlando, Fla.: Harcourt Brace Jovanovich, 1957). (Originally published 1929.)
6. Erikson, Erikson, and Kivnick, *Vital Involvement in Old Age*.

Chapter Four

1. W. H. Norman and T. J. Scaramella (eds.), *Mid-life: Developmental and Clinical Issues* (New York: Brunner/Mazel, 1980).
2. G. Sheehy, *The Silent Passage: Menopause* (New York: Random House, 1991), 85.
3. Sheehy, *Silent Passage,* 146.
4. Sheehy, *Silent Passage,* 25–26.
5. Sheehy, *Silent Passage,* 27.
6. Greenberg, *Weaving.*

Chapter Five

1. J. Campbell with B. Moyers, *The Power of the Myth* (New York: Doubleday, 1988); see also T. Parsons, "An Outline of the Social System," in T. Parsons, E. A. Shils, K. D. Naegele, and J. R. Pitts (eds.), *Theories of Society* (New York: Free Press, 1961), 30–79.
2. R. N. Bellah, R. Madsen, W. M. Sullivan, A. Swidler, and S. M. Tipton, *Habits of the Heart: Individualism and Commitment in American Life* (Berkeley: University of California Press, 1985).
3. R. Bly, *Iron John.*
4. Greenberg, *Weaving;* and C. Dowling, *The Cinderella Complex* (New York: Pocket Books, 1981).
5. See such feminist studies as Belenky and others, *Women's Ways of Knowing;* N. Chodorow, "Family Structure and Feminine Personality," in M. Z. Rosaldo and L. Lamphere (eds.), *Women, Culture and Society* (Stanford, Calif.: Stanford University Press, 1974); and Rubin, *Worlds of Pain.*
6. For women's climb up the corporate ladder, see S. Hardesty and N. Jacobs, *Success and Betrayal: The Crisis of Women in Corporate America* (New York: Franklin Watts, 1986).
7. See Greenberg, *Weaving;* E. Boulding, *The Underside of History: A View of Women Through Time* (Boulder, Colo: Westview Press, 1976); and Belenky and others, *Women's Ways of Knowing.*

8. Greenberg, *Weaving.*
9. B. Friedan, *The Feminine Mystique* (New York: Dell, 1963).

Chapter Six

1. A. de Tocqueville, *Democracy in America,* trans. George Lawrence, ed. J. P. Mayer (New York: Doubleday, 1969).
2. Bellah and others, *Habits of the Heart.*
3. W. Bennis and P. E. Slater, *The Temporary Society* (New York: HarperCollins, 1968).
4. M. E. McGill, *The 40- to 60-Year-Old Male: A Guide for Men — and the Women in Their Lives — to See Them Through the Crises of the Male Middle Years* (New York: Simon & Schuster, 1980), 100.
5. McGill, *The 40- to 60-Year-Old Male,* 100–101.
6. McGill, *The 40- to 60-Year-Old Male,* 101–102.

Chapter Seven

1. L. Kearns, *Work as a Refuge: The Sudden Death of a Child, Bereavement, and the Organization* (unpublished doctoral dissertation, The Professional School of Psychology, San Francisco, 1988).
2. Neugarten, "Continuities and Discontinuities."
3. McGill, *The 40- to 60-Year-Old Male.*
4. Greenberg, *Weaving.*
5. For example, see Gould, *Transformations; Passages: Predictable Crises of Adult Life* (New York: Bantam Books, 1977); Greenberg, *Weaving;* and Levinson and others, *The Seasons of a Man's Life.*

Chapter Eight

1. Bellah and others, *Habits of the Heart.*

Chapter Nine

1. H. S. Astin and C. Leland, *Women of Influence, Women of Vision: A Cross-Generational Study of Leaders and Social Change* (San Francisco: Jossey-Bass, 1991).

Chapter Ten

1. Erikson, Erikson, and Kivnick, *Vital Involvement in Old Age,*
    74–75.

Chapter Eleven

1. F. Popcorn, "Down-Aging," *Lear's,* September 1991, p. 130.
2. W. Bennis, *Why Leaders Can't Lead: The Unconscious Conspiracy
    Continues* (San Francisco: Jossey-Bass, 1989), 44.
3. Bennis, *Why Leaders Can't Lead,* xiii.
4. Gould, *Transformations,* 243.
5. Gould, *Transformations,* 245.
6. "Quest for Success: Male Businessmen Say Lives 'Empty,'"
    San Francisco Chronicle, March 4, 1989, p. B3.
7. G. F. Becker, "Working Women's Staunchest Allies: Sup-
    ply and Demand," *Business Week,* December 2, 1991, p. 18.

Chapter Twelve

1. P. Tillich, *Dynamics of Faith* (New York: HarperCollins,
    1977), 1–4.

INDEX

A

Achievement: attention to, 148–164; and commitment to others, 155–158; and discrimination, 152–156; factors in, 160–164; and generativity and stagnation, 159–164; and prospect of growth and change, 150–152; realism about, 148–150
Adoption, and grandparenting, 105
Adult children: in family relationships, 90, 91, 94–95, 96–97, 101–102, 106; support from, 24, 96–97, 178
Affiliation, for women, 20, 59–60
Alex, 85–86, 93, 109–110, 111, 142, 148
Allen, G., 65
American Association of Retired Persons, 2
Anima/animus guides, and inner voices, 32–34, 36
Anne, 38–39
Arlene, 107, 111, 131
Arnold, 38
Astaire, F., 65
Astin, H. S., 193
Attitudes, changing: and inner voices, 31; social, 165–167

Authenticity, and reinventing selves, 9, 168
Autonomy: and relationship, 75–88; for women, 59–63; and work, 128–130

B

Barry, 44
Beatrice, 81–82, 92
Beatty, W., 2
Becker, G. F., 193
Belenky, M. F., 32, 189, 190, 191
Bellah, R. N., 191, 192
Ben, 87–88, 92
Bennis, W., 166–167, 192, 193
Benson, 144
Berle, M., 68
Beth, 43–44, 98
Betty, 49, 96, 112, 129
Bev, 85–86
Bly, R., 56–57, 60, 189, 191
Bob, 118
Boulding, E., 191
Brenda, 42, 47
Brian, 93
Brice, F., 65
Bryan, 78
Burns, G., 65

C

Campbell, J., 55, 191
Capote, T., 8, 30, 189
Career. *See* Work and career
Caring: mutual, 26; and priorities, 20, 25; and reinventing selves, 7–8
Carol, 127
Castenada, C., 145
Castro, F., 71
Change: achievement and, 150–152; challenge of, 165–172; collaboration of men and women for, 172; for men, 167–169; openness to, 176; in social attitudes, 165–167; for women, 169–172
Charlie, 41, 101
Children. *See* Adult children
Chodorow, N., 191
Choices: and discrimination, 153–154; among priorities, 176; about work, 131–134
Cinderella Syndrome, 59
Civil rights movement, in historical context, 70
Claire, 84
Claudio, 83, 117–118, 133–134
Clinchy, B. M., 189
Collaboration, in diversity, 180
Collins, J., 2–3
Commitment to others, and achievement, 155–158
Community: and freedom, 56–59, 76; work as, 125–126
Connery, S., 165
Context: historical, 63–72; and inner voices, 32
Costner, K., 2
Crosby, B., 64
Culmination, in grandparenting, 106–108
Custer, G. A., 159
Custer, L., 159
Cynthia, 150

D

Dante, 32
Darrow, C. N., 189
David, 158
Death, and inner voices, 38–39
Deborah, 110, 140–141, 144–145

Debra, 61, 162, 163, 164
Della, 157–158
Derek, 149, 150
Dick, 130, 149, 150
Dickens, C., 30–31
DiMaggio, J., 64
Discrimination, and achievement, 152–156
Dissociation, and reinventing selves, 8
Diversity: collaboration in, 180; in fifties, 5–6; and leadership, 147
Divorce, and grandparenting, 104
Donald, 145
Donella, 42
Donna, 60
Doris, 61–62
Dreams, and priorities, 23
Dual generational demands, and priorities, 18, 22
Durocher, L., 64
Dwain, 81–82

E

Eisenhower, D. D., 68, 139, 145
Elizabeth, 148–149, 150
Ella, 157
Ellington, D., 156
Emily, 109
Empty nest syndrome, gender differences in, 98–100
Energies, focusing, 13
Entertainment industry, and historical context, 65–66
Erhard, W., 163
Erikson, E. H., 7, 12, 159, 189, 190, 193
Erikson, J., 189, 190, 193
Ethnicity: and discrimination, 154–156; in historical context, 67–68
Eunice, 52–53, 152, 153, 154
Evelyn, 16–17, 50, 150

F

Families: adult children in, 24, 90, 91, 94–95, 96–97, 101–102, 106, 178; aging parents in, 108–111; attention to roles in, 89–114; extended, 111–113; grandparenting in, 101–108; parenting in, 95–100; regrets about, 90–94;

support from, 177–178; surrogate extended, 113–114

Faye, A., 64

Fifties: attention to, 1–10; challenge of change in, 165–172; challenges and activity level in, 173–177; collaboration in, 172; conclusions on, 9–10, 181; diversities in, 5–6; external fulfillment in, 115–164; and gender differences, 3–5, 167–172; images needed for, 4–5; internal fulfillment in, 11–74; media myths about, 2–3; preparing for, 173–181; reinventing roles in, 72–74; reinventing selves in, 6–9; relationships in, 75–114; support in, 177–178; views of, 1–2, 11–13

Ford, H., 115

Fox, M. J., 2

Fred, 30, 107

Frederick, 85

Freedom, and community, 56–59, 76

Frieda, 107

Friedan, B., 71, 192

Friendship, value of, 77–80

Fulfillment: and achievement and failure, 148–164; external, 115–164; and health of body and mind, 40–54; and history, 55–74; and inner voices, 27–39; internal, 11–74; and leadership, 136–147; and priorities, 11–26; and sexuality, 43–46; work and career for, 115–135

G

Gable, C., 64

Garland, J., 65

Gay persons, relationships for, 83–84

Gender differences: in fifties, 3–5, 167–172; in parenting, 98–100; in priorities, 19–20. *See also* Men; Women

Generativity: activities for, 179–180; concept of, 7; in grandparenting, 106–108; interplay of stagnation and, 159–164; and next generation, 155–158; and priorities, 11–26

Gerald, 51, 143–144

Gilligan, C., 19–20, 189, 190

Ginsberg, A., 71

Glenda, 129

Goldberger, N. R., 189

Gould, R. L., 12, 167–168, 190, 192, 193

Grable, B., 64

Grace, 96

Grail Castles, 34–35

Grandparenting: culmination and generativity in, 106–108; joys of, 101–103; new roles in, 104–105; problems of, 103–104; surrogate, 105–106

Greenberg, E. M., 190, 191, 192

Gwen, 29–30, 31, 88

H

Hardesty, S., 191

Harriet, 81

Hayworth, R., 46

Health: attention to, 40–54; and fear of illness, 49–50; and fitness, 41–43; intellectual, 50–53; and menopause, 46–48; and pace of life, 54; and permission to act, 53–54; physical, 40–43; and relationships, 81; and sexuality, 43–46; support from, 178

History: attention to, 55–74; and context, 63–72; and cultural ungluing, 69; and entertainment industry, 65–66; and ethnicity, 67–68; images from, 64–65; and leadership, 138–140; and men's myths, 56–59; and political landscape, 68–69; and reforms, 70–71; and roles, 67, 71–74; and values, 63–64; and women's myths, 59–63; and World War II, 66–67

Hodges, G., 64

Hope, B., 65

Humanness, developing, 166–167

I

Identities, exploring alternative, 13–15

Illness, fear of, 49–50
Inner voices: attention to, 27–39; and attitude changes, 31; and context, 32; listening to, 30–31; for memories, 27–29; and men's myths, 56–59; and priorities, 13, 15, 27–29; and reinventing selves, 8–9; and relationships, 34, 36–37; sanctuaries for, 34–36; and spirituality, 37–39; and storytelling, 29–30; and success, 162; and women's myths, 61; and work expectations, 126–127
Integrity: and core values, 180–181; search for, and priorities, 25–26; to women, 20
Intimacy: and sexuality, 45; with spouse/significant other, 80–84

J

Jacobs, N., 191
Jane, 35
Jean, 17
Jerry, 117
Jill, 61
Jim, 13, 14–15, 57–58
Joan, 127
Johnson, R. A., 34, 190
Jonah, 58
José, 154, 156
Judy, 37–38
June, 76
Jung, C. G., 9, 32–34, 190

K

Karen, 85, 92–93, 117
Katherine, 102, 149, 150
Kathy Ann, 133, 134
Kean, S., 189
Kearns, L., 192
Keith, 57
Kivnick, H. Q., 189, 190, 193
Klein, E. B., 189
Kristine, 107
Kyle, 120–121

L

Larry, 129–130
Leadership: attention to, 136–147; criteria for, 137–138; and history, 138–140; opportunities for, 146–147; parental role in, 141; and political and social values, 142–145; positional, and expert power, 136–137; and priorities, 18–19, 22; valuing, 140–142; women's models for, 138, 170–171; in work and careers, 116, 146
Learning: formal and informal, 50–53; from work, 120–122
Leland, C., 193
Len, 110, 124
Levinson, D. J., 6, 189, 190, 192
Levinson, M. H., 189
Linda, 163–164
Lisa, 105
Liz, 51
Longfellow, H. W., 1, 148
Lotte, 79

M

MacArthur, D., 67
McCarthy, J., 68
McGill, M. E., 86, 192
McKee, B., 189
Madeline, 81
Madsen, R., 191
Mao Tse-tung, 71
Margaret, 85
Maria, 154, 156
Marsha, 121, 143
Martin, 126–127
Mary, 82, 94, 95, 97, 127, 158
Mary Anne, 85, 145
Mature adulthood, phase of, 7
May, 76
Mead, M., 147
Memories, inner voices for, 27–29
Men: in collaboration with women, 172; fifties for, 167–169; myths for, 56–59. See also Gender differences
Menopause, in women's lives, 46–48
Mentoring: and generativity, 155–156, 179; and partnerships, 175; by women, 171–172; in work and careers, 116
Merman, E., 65

Meuel, D., 89
Michael, 49–50
Miller, J. B., 20, 190
Millie, 102–103, 163, 164
Moral challenges, and priorities, 26
Motivations, for work, 116–120, 167–168
Myths: and history, 55–56, 59–63, 74; men's, 56–59; women's, 59–63, 100

N

Ned, 155–156
Needs, changing, 22
Neugarten, B. L., 94, 190, 192
Newman, P., 2
Noreen, 78–79
Norman, W. H., 191

P

Pace, transition of, 54
Pamela, 17, 160
Parenting: coming to terms with, 95–98; gender differences in, 98–100; leadership as, 141
Parents: aging, 108–110; work expectations from, 126–128
Parsons, T., 191
Patricia, 99
Paul, 77, 151–152
Penelope, 101
Pennsylvania, ill health in, 5
Permission to act, achieving, 53–54
Perry, 93
Politics: in historical context, 68–69; and leadership values, 142–145
Popcorn, F., 193
Porter, C., 65
Power, expert, and leadership, 136–137
Priorities: attention to, 11–26; choices among, 176; and demands, 17–19; and dreams, 23; gender differences in, 19–20; and illness, 49–50; inner voices for, 13, 15, 27–29; and integrity, 25–26; and moral challenges, 26; reordering, 15–17; struggle over, 21–22; support for reordering, 23–25

R

Rebecca, 103–104, 132
Redford, R., 2
Reese, H., 64
Reflection, time for, 169
Reinventing selves, issues in, 6–9
Relationships: attention to, 75–114; and autonomy, 75–88; in families, 89–114; with friends, 77–80; for gay persons, 83–84; and inner voices, 34, 36–37; intimacy in, 80–84; last chance for, 84–86; and priorities, 22; role models for, 76–77; support from, 177–178; tolerance in, 87–88; in youth-oriented culture, 86–87
Rena, 60–61
Retirement, and work as security, 124–125
Rita, 153–154
Roberto, 56, 78, 126, 143
Roberts, J., 2
Robinson, J., 64
Rogers, G., 65
Roles: in grandparenting, 104–105; in historical context, 67, 71–74; openness to new, 177; reversals of, 108–111
Rooney, M., 65
Roosevelt, E., 64–65
Roosevelt, F. D., 64–65
Rubin, L., 6, 189, 191
Ruth, 101

S

Sally, 127
Sam, 83–84, 132–133
Sanctuaries, for inner voices, 34–36
Sandra, 123–124
Sarah, 97
Satis, 94, 122–123
Scaramella, T. J., 191
Schopenhauer, A., 11
Security, work as, 122–125
Self-integration: achieving, 172; and inner voices, 36–37
Sexuality, and health, 43–46
Sheehy, G., 47–48, 191
Shukraft, R., 27, 29, 190

Slater, P. E., 192
Solomon, 22
Spirituality: emergence of, 181; and inner voices, 37–39
Spock, B., 96
Spouse/significant other: as friend, 78; intimacy with, 80–84; success of, 163–164; support from, 23–24
Stagnation: concept of, 7; interplay of generativity and, 159–164; and priorities, 11–26
Stories: and inner voices, 29–30; to women, 62–63
Streep, M., 2
Stress: management of, and priorities, 22; and work, 131
Sullivan, E., 68
Sullivan, W. M., 191
Support: from adult children, 24, 96–97, 178; for reordering priorities, 23–25; sources of, 177–178
Susan, 50–51, 144, 152–153, 154
Susie, 92
Suzanne, 87–88
Swidler, A., 191
Sylvia, 94, 95

T

Tarule, J. M., 189
Taylor, E., 2–3
Technology: and positional power, 137; and work, 119–120
Ted, 92
Temple, S., 65
Tillich, P., 193
Timothy, 161–162
Tina, 159–160
Tipton, S. M., 191
Tobi, 91
Tocqueville, A. de, 76, 192
Tolerance, in relationships, 87–88
Tom, 35
Tricia, 156–157
Truman, H. S., 139

V

Val, 78, 125–126
Values: common, 63–64; core, 180–181; and leadership, 147; political and social, 142–145
Veronica, 51, 101
Virgil, 136
Voices from another room. *See* Inner voices

W

Watts, A., 71, 145
Welch, R., 2–3
West Virginia, ill health in, 5
Wild Man myth, 56–58, 60
Williams, T., 76
Women: autonomy for, 59–63; in collaboration with men, 172; fifties for, 169–172; leadership models for, 138, 170–171; menopause for, 46–48; mentoring by, 171–172; myths for, 59–63, 100; professional advancement for, 170; stories to, 62–63; work roles for, 119, 127–128. *See also* Gender differences
Women's movement: and discrimination, 153–154; in historical context, 71
Woolf, V., 35, 190
Work and career: attention to, 115–135; and autonomy, 128–130; as community, 125–126; dilemmas of, 130–134; and golden handcuffs, 123; instrumental views of, 121–122; learning from, 120–122; motivations for, 116–120, 167–168; parental expectations for, 126–128; patterns of, 116, 134–135, 174–175; and reinventing selves, 7, 8; as security, 122–125; and status, 118–119, 151

Y

Young, D., 155–156
Youth-oriented culture, relationships in, 86–87

10